"Like the New York bar he joyfully pr[...] effortlessly balances high and low ae[...] precise artistry of Japanese bartending and the sunny generosity of pure hospitality. He is, in other words, both the diamond and the shine. You couldn't hope for a better guide through the intricacies and delights of Japan's many contributions to artful drinking." —ROBERT SIMONSON, *The New York Times*

"Masa says he's obsessed with serving 'surprises' to his guests. That's certainly my experience at Katana Kitten, where the Hinoki Martini arrives cradled in a wooden box, garnished to the hilt, and misted with a final aromatic spritz. He's delivered the equivalent with this book: These aren't standard drinks, but surprises, informed by deep dedication to craft and illuminated by Masa's crinkly megawatt smile."

—KARA NEWMAN, spirits editor for *Wine Enthusiast*, and author of *Cocktails with a Twist*

"A palimpsest if there ever was one, the story of the cocktail has been written, erased, and rewritten on the same sliver of land—Manhattan—for well over a century; and the author before you will leave his mark there, too. Masa Urushido's improbable journey from Nagano, Japan, to his perch at Katana Kitten on Hudson Street is one of a growing number of influential cross-pollinations between the cocktail cultures of Tokyo and Manhattan that once bred New York bars in Tokyo and Tokyo bars in Manhattan, and has gradually hybridized into an unclassified, genre-defying, Nikkei-like approach to cocktails in each city. If you read this tenderly written, beautifully photographed text by one of America and Japan's most rightfully beloved bartenders closely, I believe you'll begin to see a new way of tending bar and mixing drinks emerging—undeniably Japanese, but distinguishably American, too—like a flower blossoming improbably between the tiles of a heavily trodden sidewalk in either town."

—JIM MEEHAN, author of *Meehan's Bartender Manual* and *The PDT Cocktail Book*

"Masahiro is the best bartender I know. Scratch that, he's the best bartender any of us know. Ask any bartender who their favorite is, and Masa's name will always come up first. Every time I'm fortunate enough to be in his presence, I am constantly taking notes in an attempt to be a better bartender myself. In this book, he generously shares with us a few of the tricks that make him the best of the best."

—JEFFREY MORGENTHALER, bar manager of Clyde Tavern, co-author of *The Bar Book: Elements of Cocktail Technique* and author of *Drinking Distilled*

THE

ART OF THE

JAPANESE COCKTAIL

THE JAPANESE COCKTAIL

ART OF THE

Masahiro Urushido

AND MICHAEL ANSTENDIG

HOUGHTON MIFFLIN HARCOURT

BOSTON | NEW YORK | 2021

For information about permission to reproduce selections from this book, write to trade.permissions@hmhco.com or to Permissions, Houghton Mifflin Harcourt Publishing Company, 3 Park Avenue, 19th Floor, New York, New York 10016.

hmhbooks.com

Library of Congress Cataloging-in-Publication Data
Names: Urushido, Masahiro, author. | Anstendig, Michael, author.
Title: The Japanese art of the cocktail / Masahiro Urushido and Michael
   Anstendig.
Description: Boston : Houghton Mifflin Harcourt, 2021. | Includes
   bibliographical references and index. | Summary: "The first cocktail
   book from the award-winning mixologist Masahiro Urushido of Katana
   Kitten in New York City, on the craft of Japanese cocktail making"--
   Provided by publisher.
Identifiers: LCCN 2020023893 (print) | LCCN 2020023894 (ebook) | ISBN
   9780358362029 (hardback) | ISBN 9780358361831 (ebook)
Subjects: LCSH: Cocktails--Japan. | Cocktails.
Classification: LCC TX950.59.J3 U75 2021 (print) | LCC TX950.59.J3
   (ebook) | DDC 641.87/40952--dc23
LC record available at https://lccn.loc.gov/2020023893
LC ebook record available at https://lccn.loc.gov/2020023894

Book design by Laura Palese

Printed in the USA

1 2021
4500823691

I dedicate *The Japanese Art of the Cocktail* to my teachers and mentors in Japan and the US as an expression of my gratitude.

FOREWORD BY DAVID WONDRICH

Japanese crafts have a reputation for their discipline and their precision, and Japanese bartending is no exception. As with so many of the other crafts, though, there's a higher purpose here: Japanese bartending has a unique way of weaving the various utilitarian processes and procedures a bartender employs in mixing a drink—from opening the bottles to measuring out the ingredients to shaking, straining, garnishing, and presenting the final drink—into a seamless ritual of secular (although not entirely secular) communion. Masahiro Urushido is an exemplary ambassador for all that: To watch him mix drinks is an education in grace and elegance. Every drink of his I've had has been a thing of beauty: subtle, balanced, delicious, and presented without pretense or vanity.

But there's another side to Japanese culture, and that's the one that produced *My Neighbor Totoro* and The 5.6.7.8's; Hello Kitty and *Tampopo*. It's sweet and whimsical, warm and joyous, and it rocks. It's the culture not of the tea ceremony and the high-end cocktail bar, but of the pachinko parlor and the izakaya.

Masa is just as brilliant an ambassador for that side of Japanese culture as he is for the first one. Indeed, the thing I've always enjoyed about him is how much of that Japan he also brings to what he does, to who he is. And fortunately, with Michael Anstendig's help he has managed to work a lot of that Japan into this lovely book, tempering the rigor and precision of the craft with his characteristic warmth and generosity and playfulness. You see it in his stories, but you also see it in the drinks presented here. The drinks come from all over; from Masahiro, of course, and from other Japanese bartenders, but also from bartenders of whatever background who have been deeply inspired by Japan's drinking culture. While maintaining the characteristic Japanese attention to detail and drawing deeply from the Japanese drinks cabinet and larder, they help bring in a new energy—an exuberance not often seen in the more classic Japanese cocktail bars.

In other hands, the juxtaposition between classic and cutting-edge could seem jarring, but Masa has a way of pouring good feelings over whatever he touches, and everyone gets along as if they were sharing a round of Azusa Expresses at the bar of Katana Kitten.

PREFACE

The Japanese Art of the Cocktail was truly a journey of discovery. Getting to tell the story of Masahiro Urushido, one of the most beloved figures on the craft bartending scene, and share his invaluable mixological and cultural insights into drinks culture in Japan and the US, made this journey especially meaningful and enlightening.

My interest in Japanese culture extends far back to my college days, when I studied East Asian religions at the University of Pennsylvania. The richness of Japanese traditions, their acute attunement to the seasons and the evanescence of life, made an indelible impression on me. In the years that followed, my obsession with Japanese gastronomy, beginning with its food culture and eventually encompassing its drinks traditions, grew steadily. As a freelance writer for *Time Out New York,* I was able to share this enthusiasm and celebrate Japanese restaurants and food retailers. At the same time, I was fortunate to review a slew of New York's Japanese establishments, including some of the city's top sushi shrines, for *New York Magazine*'s website.

But none of this could prepare me for my first trip to Japan. At the time, my wife, Hanna, was representing the Akita Sake Brewers Association, and we were able to add on a few days in Tokyo together.

We hit the jackpot by hooking up with Shinji Nohara, the renowned culinary fixer who had helped Anthony Bourdain and his TV crew navigate the capital's back alleys in search of unique delicacies. From sampling restaurants specialized in a single item done to perfection to an immersion into the city's restaurant supply stores, it was nothing short of mind-boggling. And throughout, we were overwhelmed by the thoughtful and gentle hospitality. I've since returned to Japan, and each time has been a revelation for the mind and all of the senses.

So when Hanna and I came up with an idea for bringing new books to life, we were surrounded by highly talented bartenders and chefs that we wanted to help. We thought about people who had a book in them, but perhaps didn't know how to go about writing one. Masahiro Urushido was our first choice. It is an honor to be collaborating with him on our inaugural book project and his debut book.

With all the talk about Japanese bartending and the many bars that take Japan as their inspiration, we hope this book sheds some light and ignites a passion for this unique approach to drinks and to life.

—**Michael Anstendig**

INTRODUCTION

On July 24, 2018, we opened Katana Kitten, a Japanese-American bar on Hudson Street in New York City. Regarding the name, a *katana* is a samurai sword, and embodies an almost mystical level of precision and craftsmanship, and "kitten" is a nod to our sense of playfulness. The juxtaposition of these two words perfectly represents who we are. "Attention to detail" is a somewhat overused phrase in the hospitality business, but running a bar is all about timing, setting, and the entire team doing the right thing in unison. We sell food and drinks to keep the lights on and prosper, but unless we project a sense of approachability and value, we can't expect many repeat guests.

The Japanese Art of the Cocktail is the story of my journey to becoming a bartender and bar owner who embodies the Japanese approach to the cocktail, filtered through a distinctly American sensibility. It is a no-holds-barred, warts-and-all account of my growing up in a small town in the countryside of Japan, learning the ropes of hospitality and service in Tokyo, then moving to New York City and eventually opening the bar of my dreams. When I started thinking about writing this book, I grappled with defining what a Japanese bar is, and what the country's style of bartending really means. There are no

simple answers, as there are many different kinds of Japanese bars and bartending styles. Moreover, it is fascinating how the art of the cocktail, which was nurtured in the US, was transformed after its arrival in Japan. The Japanese took to the cocktail with gusto and made it their own. In a culture that ritualizes and strives to perfect art forms, from the Tea Ceremony to martial arts, it is no wonder that Japan evolved its own approach to the cocktail, an approach that was also informed by the millennia of its own drinking traditions, from sake and shochu to, more recently, whisky. Happily, Katana Kitten has resonated well with the drinking public, and it is very gratifying that our experiment in creating a truly Japanese-American bar has met with success. My goal is to demonstrate the unique contributions that this revered tradition can make to the drinks world, and what my homeland can learn in return.

Hanna Lee, president and founder of Hanna Lee Communications, a premier hospitality and travel PR agency in New York, helped launch Katana Kitten. During the process of opening the bar, she mentioned that the bar's story would make a great book. Hanna and her husband, Michael Anstendig, a freelance writer, approached me to be their debut author, with others in the pipeline. I was flattered and touched, but felt that relative to my mentors, I had a long way to go. They felt that I was in a unique position, as a bartender who straddles American and Japanese drinking traditions, to tell a unusual and personal story.

The art of the cocktail is still something that I endeavor to improve and perfect each and every day. So it is in the spirit of deep humility that I offer this book to the drinking world. I hope the insights that I share into Japan's formidable cocktail culture will benefit bartenders and libations enthusiasts the world over. I hope to inspire others to take up the mixing glass as a refined art form and a noble way of life, and to perhaps place Japan on their bucket list of transformative places to visit. *Kanpai* and cheers!

MADE IN JAPAN

I was born in Minowa, a small town in Japan's Nagano Prefecture, a landlocked region dead center in the middle of the country. The prefecture is a short train ride from Tokyo, but its stunning rusticity could not be more different than Japan's all-encompassing and dynamic capital. The region is well-known for its imposing mountains—often called the "Japanese Alps"—expansive valleys, crystal-clear lakes, and creeks, as well as lush rice paddies.

Most people are familiar with Nagano from the 1998 Winter Olympics, and many games were held in the Hakuba Valley. My family and I watched the Olympics on TV like tens of millions of other sports fans around the world, and we were very proud that the games were being held not only in Japan, but in our very own prefecture.

Like most small towns, there wasn't a lot to do in Minowa. Our options for dining out were very limited, and going to a restaurant for dinner was saved for special occasions. Our meals were cooked and eaten at home, and at a young age, I became interested in cooking, always watching and helping out in the kitchen. My maternal grandma, who lived in the nearby town of Fujimi, was an outstanding cook, and I was content to watch for hours on end as she transformed vegetables from the garden into elaborate dishes. I especially loved her fried chicken, so much so that we've immortalized it at Katana Kitten, with our own spin. My father's parents lived with us, and were constantly in their rice fields and gardens, working from sunrise to sunset and enjoying every minute of it. I began accompanying them at a young age, and helped weed the fields and harvest cucumbers and other vegetables. I will never forget the first time my grandfather had me smell a ripe tomato still attached to the vine. It made me feel a direct connection with the seasons. Many of my fondest and most profound memories of growing up in the countryside of Japan are related to smell—the scent of the fields right before it rains, the unique aromas of the seasons. These intense childhood memories are ones that I cherish and are vividly triggered whenever and wherever I encounter what, for me, are evocative scents. Looking back now, I believe that these sense memories—the flavors I encountered and the stories behind them—ended up providing me with a tremendous advantage as a bartender.

Like some kids in Minowa, I felt a bit like a country bumpkin, and I couldn't wait to grow up and move to Tokyo. While I came to love the excitement, glamour, and dynamic nature of the capital, I feel privileged to have had a country upbringing.

Something else that I discovered in my childhood was a love of making things with my hands. When I was ten, my mother took a part-time job assembling components destined for medical devices. She worked from home, and since I was skilled at making models, I loved lending her a hand. The repetition of making things exactly the same, over and over, was something that I truly enjoyed. This eye for precision and uniformity would later serve me well as a bartender, hand-carving hundreds of perfect ice spheres and cutting countless garnishes at just the right angle and all to a uniform size.

When I was fifteen, I got my first real job, working at a commercial cleaning company in Minowa. I was part of a team that would go to local supermarkets at night after they closed and scrub them clean from top to bottom. I mopped and cleaned like a devil and was handed an envelope of cash at the end of the night. (In Japan, the minimum legal working age is sixteen, so this was all under the table.) I felt enormous satisfaction at working hard, and also felt there was a dignity to it, even if it was mundane and perhaps unglamorous. To me, repetition and rituals were comforting and fulfilling, and are aspects of bartending that I cherish to this day.

I also discovered a love of the English language and all things American. My mother remembers me asking, at age four, to be enrolled in an after-school English program, as the language wasn't taught in our local elementary school. The program was run by a Japanese couple, Mr. and Mrs. Kurashima, who covered everything from the ABCs to advanced literature. I took to English immediately, and my working knowledge of the language later became my ticket to my first job in Tokyo, where my bartending journey began.

Growing up in the 1980s, American culture was pervasive in Japan and was the mark of all things cool. Movies of that era, like *Back to the Future* and *Stand by Me,* had a massive impact on me. They sparked my deep interest in America and its popular culture, especially casual clothing, like Levi's 501 jeans and Converse sneakers. This fascination would later be celebrated in the very 1980s décor of Katana Kitten.

Not everything in my Minowan childhood was idyllic. I went to a decent public school, but the educational system in Japan is driven by test scores. "Cramming then forgetting" was the standard operating procedure, with the expectation of being accepted into a good college. I got kicked out of high school in my third year for several minor infractions. My dad quickly found a private school in Tokyo that would take me in for my final year. Fortunately, the move was considered a transfer rather than an expulsion, and I earned my high school equivalency diploma. My plan was to attend a junior college for two years and transfer to a university. After the first semester, I was bored and thought it was a waste of money, so I stopped attending altogether.

It was at this time that I started bartending at karaoke bars. (And by bartending, I mean pouring beers and adding soda to commercial cocktail premixes, nothing remotely close to the kind of work I'm known for today.) I also delivered pizza, which was the best way to learn Tokyo's unforgivingly arcane and gridless streets. This was before GPS, and the delivery dispatch room in the restaurant had a huge map of Tokyo's Shibuya and Meguro neighborhoods covering one wall. (Meguro would later lend its name to our Negroni variation at Katana Kitten.) When an order came in, we would manually map it out and commit to memory all the turns we'd have to take to make it to our destination. I would often get lost and have to call in for directions. Sometimes I would just *say* I was lost, but I would actually sneak off to the rooftops of luxury condo towers to take in the breathtaking views. I would also "liberate" free pizza coupons and share them with friends who were more than happy to eat for free. It was a decent life. I'd get paid monthly on the 25th, go out partying on the 26th, and be broke before payday the following month. I was living in the moment, which was fun, but I felt unchallenged. However, fate would soon intervene and my work life would take a new direction.

One day when I was nineteen, I was riding on the Tōyoko subway line with my girlfriend at the time. She had a copy of *From A,* which is basically a compendium of help-wanted ads, and asked me to put my finger on a page she randomly flipped to, without looking. I did, and found myself pointing to an ad for a food runner position at Tableaux, one of Tokyo's hottest fine-dining restaurants at the time, whose clientele included celebrities, actors, and well-to-do expats. The job required someone who spoke English, and the photo accompanying the ad made the restaurant look like a gorgeous storybook castle,

so I decided to give it a go. I was interviewed first by phone and was then asked to come to the restaurant. Once there, I was interviewed by a manager, along with eight other candidates. We each gave our names and recited our work experience. Many of the others had serious credentials from working in renowned fine-dining restaurants, and knew about wine. When it came to me, I was pretty nervous, as my experience had been karaoke bars. I was an absolute beginner and, happily, it worked in my favor.

Tableaux thrust me into the magical, rarefied, and slightly terrifying world of uniformed waiters, double tablecloths, Goldman Sachs expense accounters, and the occasional rock star. It was the flagship dinner-restaurant concept of Global-Dining's Kozo Hasegawa, a visionary who built an empire from a single café to many venues. His right-hand man was Yoshihiro Shinkawa, who had built and ran the day-to-day operations of all their venues.

The smell of buttery, oven-fresh pastries and rich sauces pervaded the restaurant, which served a contemporary hybrid of French and Italian cuisines using local Japanese ingredients. There were other global influences, including Spago-inspired California cuisine, as well as an enormous list of French, Italian, and Californian wines. I was enchanted, but everything was new and confusing. It was the first time that I had seen bottled water like San Pellegrino. I wondered why someone would drink water from halfway around the world and pay so much for it when they could get water for free from the faucet. I had to learn hundreds of new vocabulary terms that were

completely alien to me. Who knew there was a specific word to describe the spoon used to serve fish? For the first time in my life, I felt seriously challenged and was very aware that other people's reputations were now depending on me.

For each shift, I'd start by cleaning the bathroom and polishing mountains of silverware. The waiters sauntered in 30 minutes before service began. They were rock stars in their own special waiter jackets with freshly pressed white shirts and ties. They were super cool, but quite intimidating.

I also had to master the intricacies of formal place settings and the many varieties of Western silverware and cutlery. Each had its own exact position on the table, yet to me they were virtually indistinguishable, especially for someone who, until then, had only known simple forks, knives, spoons, and, of course, chopsticks. I was overwhelmed, but undaunted. After three months, I could identify each piece with my eyes closed, just by its weight. My tasks were intense and grueling, picking up heavy tubs of dirty dishes, restocking endless bottles of water, running food to tables and serving the plates in the proper order by differentiating the table's hosts from their guests, mapping out timings of service, and making sure each table, from intimate two-tops to large parties, was properly set and ordered. It was nerve-racking, and it took a long time to enjoy what I was doing.

While I had always thought—and still think—that my grandmother's cooking was the best thing I ever ate, suddenly I was encountering filet mignon and foie gras, which proved to be revelatory experiences for me. The restaurant also had a private dining room, which had its own discreet subterranean entrance used by celebrities, like Mick Jagger, when the Rolling Stones were in town to perform. As a food runner, I was tasked with cleaning up the room after the guests departed. I quickly saw that they were leaving behind significant quantities of jaw-droppingly expensive wine. My wine education began by furtively sneaking sips of some of the world's greatest wines, including *grand vins* like Chateau Latour 1982, my birth year, and great California wines, like Opus One, that had been left on the tables in the private dining room. Not a bad way to learn about wine!

The atmosphere was extremely competitive, even by Japanese standards. But soon one of the bartenders quit, and a bar back position opened up. I enjoyed running food every night, but I was up for a new challenge. Again, I was thrust into a foreign universe. I didn't recognize a single bottle behind the bar, which was an encyclopedic collection of Western spirits, from whiskies to brandies and cordials to grappas. I had zero knowledge of classic cocktails, let alone how to make them.

I spent much of my time washing and polishing hundreds of wine and cocktail glasses and burnishing the bottles behind the bar, which contained spirits that were easily worth more than my weekly salary. Luckily, my first sensei, Yasushi Torisawa, the restaurant's bar manager, took me under his wing as my mentor and teacher. His background was working in hotel bars, and he was a master of classic stirring and shaking techniques. My education was gradual. Torisawa-san was hands-on in his instruction and sampled each of my drinks by dipping his barspoon in my shaker, then placing a few drops on top of his fist to taste. Only if they passed muster would they be allowed to be sent to the tables.

One of the most challenging tasks to master was carving perfect ice spheres from ice blocks with a single-pronged ice pick. I learned by watching and eventually carving dozens of spheres before each shift, as well as many more during service. Torisawa-san gave me tips on how to hold the ice, the trajectory necessary to sheer off just the right amount of ice, how to rotate the ball methodically to ensure perfect symmetry, and, perhaps most important, how to avoid stabbing my hand with the pick, which I did many times. I was struck by the amount of work and dedication it took to create something so fleeting that would soon melt away in a guest's glass, yet provide that guest with great pleasure.

Still, the pace was intense and I often fell behind in my duties. At one point, I was in the proverbial weeds and head waiter Tomoaki Asai screamed at the general manager that I was stupid, too young for the position, and incapable of getting the job done. Asai-san eventually recognized my earnest efforts and how was learning and trying to do things right. Slowly, he began giving me compliments and ultimately became my primary sensei. That gave me a great sense of achievement, and we eventually became good friends, with him even taking me out for drinks after work, despite the generation gap. He's considered a legend in Tokyo's dining scene and is one of the best maître d's I have ever met.

Shinkawa-san, our COO, would actually take a shift every Friday night, which was when he earned the nickname "God of Service." This really inspired us, especially observing his interactions with our guests.

After a few years, I started recognizing our regulars and developed a skill to anticipate their needs, even before they realized they needed something. The team noticed this and appreciated my forethought. I studied our guests' likes and their habits, whether they drank with their left hand or right, and I mastered the art of swiftly changing ashtrays after every cigarette was snuffed out, without being noticed by the guests.

The restaurant closed at around midnight, earlier than most neighboring venues, and at Tableaux Lounge, a cigar bar located next door that rocked until four a.m., I saw an opportunity to earn a little extra cash and gain more experience. I was soon taken under the wing of its famed charismatic bartender, Yasuyuki "Antonio" Suzuki. Antonio-san was nicknamed after Hollywood heartthrob Antonio Banderas, because women loved him and men admired him. He had built an incredible following of regulars, thanks to his superb cocktails and his ability to pick up conversations with guests from visit to visit, right where they had been left off, even if months or years had passed. Antonio-san was also a master of managing the flow of the room and jumping out from behind the bar to help bus tables or personally greet one of his favorite guests.

During my time at Tableaux, fate would intercede yet again. My cousin Hiroshi had been a regular fixture at our family events when I was growing up, and because his family lived a bit closer to Tokyo, he was immediately way cooler than me. After he moved to New York City to get his graduate degree in architecture and interior design, he invited me to visit him, and I jumped at the chance. It was 2003, and Anthony Bourdain's breakout memoir *Kitchen Confidential* had already burned up the bestseller list.

So I found myself gleefully couch-surfing at my cousin's apartment in Sunnyside, Queens. During the day I would go sightseeing, and at night I would visit fine-dining spots like Veritas, wd-50, Stanton Social, Allen & Delancey, Gotham Bar & Grill, and Ouest. That first trip to New York turned into an annual visit, and after a while, Hiro-chan suggested that I relocate to the city and attend college. Of course, the idea immediately appealed to me.

Meanwhile, back in Tokyo, there were major developments taking place at Tableaux. The restaurant's COO, Shinkawa-san, announced that he was leaving the company to start his own restaurant group. I learned that Asai-san and other top in-house talent were already joining him in his new venture, and Shinkawa-san made me a job offer as well. The new restaurant, Dazzle, was a modern fine-dining concept with very upscale architecture and a prime Ginza location. I was offered complete control of the bar program and drink development. It was, as they say, an offer I couldn't refuse, but I made sure to let Shinkawa-san know that it would be short-term, as moving to New York was on my horizon.

At first, as I delved into creating and running the bar program, Dazzle captured my imagination. It was a big step up for me. Working under Shinkawa-san and Asai-san and having them allow me to do this was thrilling. I soon got into the rhythm of working in Ginza and going out after work with Asai-san to our favorite *tachinomi* (standing bars). I continued to learn and grow, but my goal remained to go to New York City and attend college.

When my grandfather passed away in 2007, I took it as a sign that it was time for a change.

I ended up moving to New York City in the spring of 2008 and started my first semester at LaGuardia Community College in Long Island City in pursuit of an associate degree in hospitality management. I was on my own, without any financial support from my family. Thanks to my very first friend in New York, Paul Franich, I landed a job at Kingswood, a high-volume bar in Greenwich Village where I first demonstrated my ice carving skills and got to work with a diverse team, and later, at Ruby's Cafe, a casual Australian coffee shop owned by the same group.

The most important part of working at Kingswood was meeting my future wife, Taryn. She walked into the bar one day to meet a friend, and I was immediately attracted at the first sight of her. Her office was just a few blocks away from Ruby's Cafe, so she was there quite often, and whenever she came to visit, I would give her free coffee and never charged her anything for food. (Sometimes you have to break some rules for the sake of love.) We quickly found that we enjoyed the same things. We both loved family and creativity, going to the park and cooking together, and we spent time enjoying the seasons of New York. Those were the greatest days of my life, and I knew we were meant to be together.

It was around that time that Naren Young reached out to me and offered me a job at the soon-to-open Saxon + Parole. An Australian-born veteran of New York City's bar scene, Naren had worked at top craft cocktail bars and restaurants with renowned bar programs like Pegu Club, The Dutch, Bobo, and Locanda Verde. I was flattered, but frankly, I was doing well at Kingswood. He eventually won me over and soon I was at Saxon + Parole, a high-volume restaurant and bar on the Bowery, about a month after it opened.

Thanks to Naren, I met everyone in the industry. Working at Saxon + Parole was like going back to school again. I had a lot to catch up on, including making and working with housemade infusions, syrups, and seasonal fresh fruits and vegetables. Naren changed the course of my drink-making career. He was passionate about the history of the cocktail and the fact that every classic drink has a story. He brought these narratives to life and related how history influences contemporary times. I definitely consider Naren an important sensei, and he has had a profound influence on my life.

It was at Saxon + Parole that I first met Ignacio Jimenez, a larger-than-life and infectiously charismatic figure affectionately known as "Nacho." He would come to have a profound impact on how I evolved as a bartender and, ultimately, how I define my bartending style. So much of what I have achieved I owe to Nacho. It all traces back to working every single brunch shift together in the beginning, cementing our bond of friendship for life. In 2012, Naren and Nacho were opening The Daily, a sister bar to Saxon + Parole located adjacent to the restaurant PUBLIC. The concept there was a pre-Prohibition classic cocktail menu that literally changed every day. Because of the intensity and demands of the program, we really immersed ourselves re-creating drinks from vintage cocktail books and Naren's

recipe Rolodex. I had a lot to learn. And at the same time, I was enjoying all of my shifts with the bar team at Saxon + Parole, which went on to win "World's Best Restaurant Bar" at Tales of the Cocktail in 2013.

Naren eventually offered me the job of bar manager at Saxon + Parole, and I shifted the majority of my working days back to the bar. Soon after, he decided to move on to new projects, and I inherited a bar with an incredibly strong concept. The bar went on to win "Best American Restaurant Bar" at Tales of the Cocktail in 2016. But while I was thrilled, especially for the bar team, it didn't feel like I could put my own stamp on the bar.

That tells you a little bit about my life leading up to Katana Kitten. I never imagined being a bartender, moving to New York, and making it my home, never devised a plan and followed a precise career path to bring me to these auspicious moments in time. To be honest, a lot of it came down to the work ethic and moral code instilled in me by my family and mentors I found along the way, being gracious about opportunities, and quite a bit of good luck. But looking back, I can now see how all these elements came together seamlessly, and much better than I ever could have planned, or frankly, even imagined.

THE YEAR OF THE KITTEN

The impetus for opening a new kind of Japanese bar in New York City goes to my partner, James Tune. He's still the general manager of Boilermaker, a highly successful bar in Manhattan's East Village dedicated to, as the name implies, boilermakers, among other classic cocktails. James had come up in the city's craft cocktail scene, having managed the legendary craft cocktail den Pegu Club for many years after an earlier spin working in nightlife. He had become obsessed with *Kill Bill,* the epic Quentin Tarantino movie starring Uma Thurman as a wronged assassin on a path of revenge, whose preferred weapon is a custom, hand-forged *katana,* a classic samurai sword. James reached out to me through our mutual friend, Kenta Goto, and we met at Boilermaker, where James is a partner with Greg Boehm. Greg is the founder of Cocktail Kingdom, the barware and cocktail book boutique in Manhattan's NoMad neighborhood that's become an essential resource for bartenders globally and made Japan's sublime barware ubiquitous in craft cocktail bars around the world. A third-generation publisher, Greg's first claim to fame was launching Mud Puddle Inc., where he reprinted rare and important out-of-print tomes penned by the illuminati of the first golden age of the cocktail: Jerry Thomas, Harry Johnson, Harry McElhone, and Hugo Ensslin. While these exquisite and foundational books had once been the exclusive province of well-to-do collectors, thanks to Mud Puddle, now anyone could readily afford them. This played a pivotal role in reacquainting US bartenders with pre-Prohibition cocktails and classic techniques that had been essentially lost to time. He and his team have gone on to create Cocktail Kingdom Hospitality Group, which, in addition to Boilermaker, is behind such acclaimed New York bars as Existing Conditions with Dave Arnold and Don Lee; Mace with Nico de Soto; The Cabinet, a cozy rye and mezcal destination; and the Christmas-themed Miracle and Sippin' Santa pop-ups, which have more than a hundred participating bars across the US and internationally.

James sketched out his concept in general terms, and mentioned that he already had a space in mind. Swine, a bar in the West Village on Hudson Street, had fallen on hard times, and the owner was looking to move out of the city. Of course, with real estate at such a premium in Manhattan, this was no small thing. James also had Greg's financial backing as a partner, another major advantage. I immediately loved the space and saw endless possibilities with the bilevel room that could support a single concept on both floors, or two very different ones

on each. It also had a working kitchen. I was all in. Things quickly fell into place, and our official partnership was formed in July 2017. Our basic concept was a full-throttle Japanese-American bar. Not a Japanese bar in New York, not a Japanese-inspired or -themed bar, but rather a hybrid of two formidable drinking cultures, with each given equal respect and prominence.

We wanted to create a bar that married the casual carousing vibe found in izakaya with the precision encountered in Japan's formal cocktail bars, all with the warm familiarity of a local New York neighborhood bar. The goal was to be accessible to as many people as possible as "everyone's everyday bar." This entailed a wide array of drink offerings, from straightforward boilermakers to a high-concept martini to our twist on classic cocktails. And of course there would be highballs. Lots of highballs.

We took over Swine's lease, as well as their liquor license, and it was game on. As partners, each of us brought a deep passion about Japan to the project, and everyone had their own clearly defined role and point of view. I was in charge of creating Katana Kitten's identity, developing its cocktail menu, and steering the direction of the culinary program. I would also recruit, train, and manage the team; orchestrate the style of service; and direct the overall approach to hospitality.

Greg was a frequent visitor to Japan and drank in more than seventy local bars, more than any non-Japanese person I had ever met. In addition, Greg has a superb private collection of rare Japanese whiskies, which only a few have been lucky to see, let alone sip.

And lastly, James was a Japanophile through and through. His exposure to the country and its aesthetic via popular culture had unleashed an unquenchable thirst to learn and experience everything he could about Japan. He would manage the day-to-day operations. When we negotiated the contract, I insisted that we take James to Japan. He had never been, and I felt very strongly that he had to see Tokyo's legendary drinks scene firsthand. I wanted to provide him with a total immersion education as part of our R&D, so James and I jetted off to Tokyo.

Our itinerary was immersive and intensive. I wanted him to experience every kind of drinking and eating establishment, from the refined bars of Ginza to the highly personal and exuberant watering holes of Golden Gai and everything in between. The goal was to give James a frame of reference and a library of his own sense memories. Once back in New York City, we set off to pull together the ultimate bar team that we thought would understand what we were trying to achieve at Katana Kitten.

When I discussed the idea with my now-wife, Taryn, she immediately suggested I call Laura McGinley, a top-notch bartender who paints in her spare time. Happily, Laura, a friend and colleague of mine, came to join our team full-time. We had worked together at PUBLIC when I was at the adjacent bar, The Daily. At PUBLIC, she had distinguished herself in every imaginable position, from bartender to host to maître d' to manager. Her sweet, bright charm is infectious, and she immediately puts people at ease with her smile. It doesn't matter who you are or where you are from—everyone who comes to the bar gets the exact same treatment. She makes it clear that she is there to take care of you. Plus, Laura has an amazing work ethic and is supremely punctual, something that is very important behind the bar.

She also introduced me to Abeo Miller, who was working with her at the time at Dudley's, owned by the Kingswood folks. Abeo was the very first person that I interviewed. He had lived in Japan as a young boy, an experience that had made a profound impression on him. Abeo had worked at Maison Premiere, an acclaimed, elegant bar in Williamsburg, Brooklyn, as well as at Locanda Verde, Chef Andrew Carmellini's popular Tribeca taverna. I was impressed with his fine-dining background, which really makes you understand the importance of the various steps of service, the varying levels of formality, and why you do things a certain way. Besides being a very talented bartender, he is one of the hardest-working people in the business. He started part-time and always supported our vision for Katana Kitten. He is now behind the bar full-time and, thanks to his hard work and engagement with our guests, has risen to head bartender.

I was also lucky to learn that Nana Shimose-gawa, the bar manager of Angel's Share, the highly influential Japanese-inspired cocktail bar in Manhattan's East Village, was leaving her position. When I reached out to her, she immediately signed on. From the get-go, we wanted an international and diverse bar team. After all, Katana Kitten is a Japanese-American bar, and it was important for me to have Japanese bartenders working alongside me. I had known Nana-san for a long time, and she had distinguished herself at Angel's Share, where she worked with bar star Shingo Gokan, who now has several top bars in Tokyo and Shanghai. Nana is quiet and gentle, but very focused; she has a strong presence and exudes an unmistakable sense of confidence. The way she makes drinks is absolutely beautiful to watch.

Also on our radar was Kodai Yamada. His distinguished personality and rockabilly pompadour make it hard to miss Kodai. Greg Boehm spoke extremely highly of him and sent me to watch him behind the bar at Hi-Collar, an East Village coffee shop by day and sake bar by night. They also serve shochu, beer, and some food, but not much in the way of cocktails. But the real reason people went there was to see Kodai and socialize with him. He has an uncanny ability to create genuine relationships with bar guests. Kodai had trained as a bartender in Japan before moving to New York City. He helped open Hi-Collar, and soon became the face of the bar. Upon meeting Kodai for the first time, I was immediately impressed by his politeness, exuberant style, and deep knowledge of sake. When James Tune and I initially approached him to join Katana Kitten, he demurred, saying that his bar needed him. We were impressed by his loyalty, but we persisted. By the fourth offer, he agreed to come on board once a week. This has since evolved into a full-time position, and we couldn't be happier. He is in charge of every single housemade cordial at the bar, and keeps them completely fresh and consistent, which is no small task. He is our sake sommelier, and a gentle soul who takes care of every guest in the same thoughtful way.

Also joining our team was Lalo Hernandez, one of the best bartenders I have ever known. I like to say that Lalo has a Buddha-like sense of calm. No matter how crazy things get at Katana Kitten, no matter how demanding guests can be, Lalo never loses his cool. That is a real testament to his strong character. His demeanor never changes, no matter who he is serving. We met when he was behind the stick at Ghost Donkey, a high-energy tequila-fueled bar around the corner from Saxon + Parole, its sister bar. He was working with Nacho, who encouraged him to be a part of Katana Kitten, knowing that he would be a quintessential part of the opening team. Since day 1, we continue to be impressed by his work ethic; he is never late and seldom, if ever, gets sick.

We were also lucky to land Armando Cortez, a highly charismatic bartender who embodies warm hospitality. Armando is a rising star. He was a regular guest at Ghost Donkey, and I remembered him sitting at the bar and having a vibrant smile that I will never forget. We needed a solid bar back, so on Lalo's recommendation, we approached Armando. He had been working at a Mexican restaurant's bar and was loyal to his team. Eventually, he agreed to join us, and showed up at Katana Kitten on the first day of training. He was a superb bar back and was

eventually promoted to bartender. Armando has an almost preternatural sense of anticipating what a guest needs before the guest even asks for it or perhaps even thinks of it. That is a real skill, and one that is extremely difficult to develop. It's very intuitive. Equally important, Armando understands me and my obsession with serving "surprises" to our guests. It is all about the timing, when to pull out a small surprise or a big one or one that is just a little bit weird and charmingly puzzling.

As general manager, we were fortunate to have Jordis Unga join us. An accomplished professional singer and musician, the extroverted Jordis is beloved by the team for her caring attitude. Jordis curates Katana Kitten's awesome rock, soul, and disco playlists and often plays her guitar prior to her shifts in our downstairs bar as her own way of meditating.

With our team in place, we turned our attention to the really challenging part: creating the all-important cocktail menu. My drinks are always grounded in classic cocktails and imbued with seasonality. After that, I endeavor to inject uniquely Japanese ingredients, traditions, and rituals into each and every drink. The cocktail menu consists of fifteen drinks divided into three sections: five highballs, to salute Japan's most popular drink style; five signature cocktails that pay homage to the classics, with a Japanese twist; and five boilermakers, to show respect for our sister bar that was partly James's inspiration for Katana Kitten.

Since we have been open for a relatively short while, we are still working our way toward finding out what our guests like and expect from Katana Kitten. The top three highballs and signature cocktails never leave the menu. The last two slots are switched out to showcase much more seasonal libations, and daily and weekly drink specials are written out on the back bar's mirror. You'll also find a hand-scrawled proclamation from cocktail historian David Wondrich, which he shared after his first visit, praising our highballs and calling them "The Coldest 'balls in the City!"—one of my favorite quotes.

Beyond the cocktails, the culinary offerings at Katana Kitten were very important to us. My intention was to bring in the traditional Japanese food you might find at an izakaya and merge it with popular American bar food. I was fortunate to collaborate with Cocktail Kingdom Hospitality Group's culinary team, including Chef Nick Sorrentino and Chef Cyed Adraincem, to bring the concept to life.

The transformation of Swine into Katana Kitten entailed about four months of construction and renovations. The all-important interior design was a collaboration between Jason Volenec, a leading interior designer, and Jeannette Kaczorowski, who is creative director of Cocktail Kingdom and does the detailed interior design for the group's sister bars. As it happened, Volenec had designed Swine, so he was intimately familiar with our space. He is a big fan of Japanese culture and has visited the country many times, including the famed Golden Gai, with its myriad of tiny yet highly expressive bars.

For inspiration, Volenec looked to the Taishō era, Japan's Jazz Age, which immediately followed the Meiji era, when Japan opened to the world. During the Meiji era the Japanese encountered new ways of living, which they viewed as curiosities to be kept at a distance. It wasn't until the Taishō era, and the generation after Meiji, when the culture shifted and ordinary Japanese began incorporating outside tastes in fashion, music, food, and drink into their daily lives. This was seen in Taishō architecture as well, with houses of the time sporting prominent beams, something Volenec spotlighted at Katana Kitten's upstairs bar.

The upstairs is also plastered with an extensive collection of Japanese posters from the 1970s and '80s, which is when Greg Boehm, James Tune, and I all came of age. Throughout the last century, the US had an enormous cultural impact on Japan, and I grew up watching US films like *The Goonies.* We have Japanese posters of American movies—everything from *Saturday Night Fever* to *Taxi Driver* to *Star Wars* and *Back to the Future.* There are also '80s posters promoting Japanese rock bands and a collection of Japanese ads, both vintage and reprints, that are all part of Greg Boehm and Jeannette Kaczorowski's personal collection.

Downstairs, the inspiration is purely Golden Gai. The objective was not to create a facsimile, but to imagine what the concept would look like transposed to New York City. These diminutive bars epitomize organized chaos, and are filled with decorations and knickknacks that express the owners' personalities, interests, and hobbies on every square inch of wall space and shelving. It takes them years to build up this level of visual impact. Guests sit communally, and there is something special about eating and drinking with strangers in Japan. At Katana Kitten, we incorporated Japanese posters, a miso brewery ad from my hometown of Minowa, as well as a vintage 1974 Sammy Davis Jr. Suntory ad with the slogan, "I Say Suntory."

Our collection is constantly growing, with souvenirs from Japan and ephemera from offsite events and pop-ups added on a regular basis. Thanks to the kitchen downstairs, the room is filled with homey cooking aromas, which greet our guests and have them immediately reaching for the food menu. To further create a mood, we added a projector to display classic Japanese films, like Akira Kurosawa's *Seven Samurai,* incomprehensibly weird Japanese game shows, and sporting events. Luckily, every seat has a great view.

The final piece of the puzzle was to get the word out. Greg Boehm reached out to Hanna Lee, whose agency, Hanna Lee Communications, helped make The Dead Rabbit a household name. I personally related to Hanna, since she had grown up in South Korea, and like me, threw caution to the wind and moved to New York City to pursue her dream. She is an unstoppable ball of energy and knows literally everyone in the cocktail scene, as well as key media. Her husband, Michael Anstendig, is an accomplished journalist who is also an obsessive home bartender. I was thrilled to work with them to tell Katana Kitten's story.

At the same time, on the personal side, Taryn and I were planning a family of our own. The way we had it timed was for our new baby to arrive just as we were opening the bar. However, childbirth is a more predictable process than opening a bar in New York City. Due to construction delays, we were delighted to welcome little Azusa into the world on her actual due date, eight months before Katana Kitten opened.

Opening Katana Kitten was a labor of love and a genuine expression of my journey as a bartender from Japan to the US, full of inspiration from my mentors and friends, and with a strong partnership with Greg, James, and the team. We are very proud that the bar has resonated with our guests and earned wide acclaim. Even without these humbling awards, which exceeded any of our expectations, it would all have been worth it.

THE JAPANESE WAY OF THE COCKTAIL

The cocktail arrived in Japan not long after Commodore Perry's gunboats pried the country open to trade with the US. Japan had spent centuries in self-imposed isolation, and the port city of Yokohama was the first to welcome American traders and their new-fangled wonders, including the camera, steam power, and, most spiritedly, whiskey. By the 1860s, it was in the Yokohama Hotel that Westerners slaked their thirst at Japan's first bar serving spirits, beer, and wine. Everything was poured straight up, and the Wild West atmosphere featured a rowdy clientele prone to firing their pistols at the bar's wall clock. The hotel was walled off to keep the outsiders out of view of prowling samurai, who took a dim view of the newly arrived interlopers.

It would be another decade before proper cocktails made their first appearance in Japan, debuting at Yokohama's International Hotel in 1874. Meanwhile, stateside, Jerry Thomas was reigning supreme as the father of American mixology, and the first golden age of the cocktail was in all its glory. In 1890, German-born Louis Eppinger arrived at Yokohama's Grand Hotel, a spot that got high marks from Rudyard Kipling. Eppinger is widely credited with introducing cocktails, like the Bamboo and the Million Dollar,

to Japan. While his guests were foreigners, the bar team was local and proved to be eager acolytes.

The Japanese were fast to catch on. Kamiya Bar in Tokyo's Asakusa neighborhood opened in 1880 and became known for its signature drink, Denki Bran, which is still served today. Translated as "electric brandy," it was an easy-to-drink concoction made from inexpensive fruit brandy, sweet claret wine, and a blend of herbs. The Western-inspired food on the menu at Kamiya Bar is also grounded in history. They still serve a version of the menu that was in place when they opened during the Meiji Restoration, with renditions of spaghetti and hamburgers.

While the Meiji Restoration introduced Japan to foreign influences, it wasn't until the Taishō era of the 1920s that this influence trickled down to everyday Japanese. Often compared with the free-wheeling Jazz Age in America, this period was when cocktails really entered Japan's modern vocabulary. In Ginza, Western-style cafés and bars proliferated, many of them staffed by veterans of the Grand Hotel who had benefited from Eppinger's tutelage. Others had gained experience on the high seas by working on luxury ocean liners. In 1926, *Kokuteeru*, Japan's first cocktail book with detailed recipes and

Western measurements, was published by Yonekichi Maeda.

Following World War II, cocktails fell out of popularity until Japan once again enjoyed prosperity. And when they returned, they returned with a vengeance, appealing to both men and women. The modern phenomenon was spurred by Suntory with the opening of thousands of Torys Bars across Japan, catering to rank-and-file Japanese. While fairly cookie-cutter, the bars' uniformity of experience was reassuring and built a loyal following, much like any modern franchise. Luxury bars were now on the defensive, and their bartenders mastered new techniques, most notably impeccably carved ice, to justify their high prices.

As a partner and "Director of Deliciousness" of Katana Kitten, my dream-come-true Japanese-American bar in New York City's West Village, I am frequently asked to define Japanese bartending and its unique style. The question is one that I constantly grapple with, as there is no simple answer. Clearly, it involves many touchstones, from the use of specialized bar tools to specific techniques and curated ingredients. But it is much more profound than that.

My own approach to Japanese bartending was gleaned from my mentors in Tokyo, yet was highly influenced by Naren Young, who took me under his wing in New York and taught me American bartending. There is a celebration of working clean and of paying attention to the temperature of the room. As anyone who works in service, I always try to put myself in the guests' shoes. I make a point of carefully reading

the mood of my guests by seeking out clues in their gestures and eye contact. Learning guests' habits and preferences is essential, and forms the basis of anticipating their needs later on.

Another unique standard is the popularity of the three-piece cobbler shaker, with the strainer built into the lid, rather than the two-piece tin set or Boston shaker that is popular the world over.

As I trained as a bartender in Japan, I came to see the repetitive routines and rituals of pre-service preparation, service, and post-service cleanup as an essential everyday meditation. It helps to ensure that the drinks we serve are served the same way to every guest, and that each drink is as identical as humanly possible. Since the routine contains elements that are duplicated every day, when something is wrong or out of place, it is immediately noticeable and can be fixed.

I personally learned the bartending trade in Japan through traditional apprenticeships. The mode of teaching was called *minarai,* which roughly translates to "watch and learn," or learning by observation. It was an arduous process. The lack of formal instruction forced me to understand the processes on my own and correlate that with the physical skills of bartending. There was not much spoon-feeding of instruction. By trying to figure things out myself, including the hows and the whys, I gained a deeper understanding than I would had if the insights had simply been bestowed upon me.

As with any trade, bartending is difficult to learn from just reading books. The instruction has to be hands-on. In many Japanese bars, there are very limited spots for apprentices, and the positions are attained through hard-core networking. I was extremely lucky that a bartending path opened up to me at the ideal time in my life. I had only been to one cocktail bar in my life before that. I didn't think it was all that good, and I had to pretend I actually liked the drink I was served.

When I was growing up, Japanese culture placed a premium on staying at the same job for a long time. My dad joined Seiko Epson at age eighteen as a quality-control engineer and stayed on the job for thirty-six years. In New York City, I have seen bartenders hop around and juggle multiple part-time positions. There is an advantage to this, as it helps spread bartending knowledge and techniques among many bars, rather than keep it siloed. In my experience in Japan, if a bartender left a position after a short period, their credibility could potentially be compromised. Moreover, moving from one Japanese bar to another is very difficult to pull off. The new bar will insist that the bartender learn the new venue's particular way of making drinks. But at a certain point, once Japanese bartenders have enough experience, many take the plunge and open their own bars, where they can practice and perfect their preferred style of service.

In many traditional Japanese arts, like gardening, architecture, or interior design, minimalism is the driving aesthetic. "Less is more" is something that inspires our cocktails at Katana Kitten, as well as our bar snacks. Every single ingredient and garnish in each drink has to be aligned with its overall concept. We are constantly trying to cut out any "extras" to find the immutable essence of the cocktail. The challenge is to express and deliver a memorable experience to our guests, with the absolute minimum of distracting elements.

My love and respect for Japanese bartending is infinite, and having now worked outside Japan for more than a decade, I can view it more objectively. While my native land and its obsession with perfection has much to teach the bartending world, I can also see areas where it can learn from the wider global drinks community.

The other aspect of Japanese bartending is reliability. Across the board, Japanese bars consistently, and without fail, deliver what is expected. There is something absolutely comforting in a timeless experience, and you can find that in cocktail bars throughout Japan.

Japanese bartending's reverence for tradition and ritualization still leave room for experimentation, innovation, and *kaizen,* which means "continuous improvement." While the practices might appear the same, they have been arrived at through well-considered and time-tested methods. This self-motivated perfectionism and meticulousness pervades Japanese culture.

I find it very exciting to see non-Japanese bartenders embrace and experiment with Japanese ingredients in their cocktails. Japanese bartenders definitely incorporate quintessential ingredients, like *sakura* (cherry blossoms), yuzu (a citrus fruit), and shiso (a fresh herb), but generally do so in predictable ways. This is because they have a set of established associations and expectations for how they should be used, along with the specific memories the ingredients conjure. Non-Japanese bartenders do not have this conceptual legacy, and approach the ingredients as a blank canvas for their unbridled creativity.

Today, the concept and practice of sustainability has become prevalent in the contemporary bartending world and in society at large. I've long been inspired by Iain Griffiths and Kelsey Ramage and their work for Trash Tiki, where they make cordials from spent lime or lemon husks and use other "upcycling" methods. This resonates deeply with me, as in Japan there is a strong cultural bias against waste. It is a combination of a culture that reveres nature and pays respect to every form of life, no matter how humble. Moreover, in the postwar era of deprivations and austerity, waste was simply unthinkable and unacceptable from a practical standpoint. The habits formed during those trying years became habits

for life, regardless of the country's actual state of prosperity, and even influenced later generations.

My own grandmother would carefully wrap and save even the smallest piece of ginger and thoughtfully place it in the refrigerator. Never mind that she might forget about it—she always had the right intention. A certain degree of sustainability and waste minimization are hardwired into Japanese culture. I feel privileged that I learned this sensibility from my grandmother over years and years.

It has been an absolutely thrilling opportunity to open Katana Kitten, a bar that synergistically brings together the best of Japanese and American styles of bartending. From Japan, we bring exactitude and a relentless quest for perfection, a respect for classic cocktails, combined with selfless hospitality. Into this, we infuse a decidedly American penchant for diverse creativity, unique housemade and garden-fresh ingredients, and a touch of playfulness. But, at the end of the day, despite all our good intentions, it is up to the drinking public to decide if our noble experiment will flourish.

UNDERSTANDING JAPAN'S DRINKING CULTURE:
SAKE, SHOCHU, AND JAPANESE WHISKY

Growing up in Minowa, the only times I saw hard alcohol served were at seasonal gatherings I attended with my family. The heads of the community households, including my father and grandfather, would gather together to mark the seasons, and food was always served, as well as beer and sake. At times, the gathering would be held over the weekend and everyone turned out for it, including all the kids, as there were no babysitters to watch us. It was on these occasions when tipsy fathers, my own included, would let their kids, me included, have their first sip of beer or sake.

Beer and sake were fixtures at every formal family gathering, from weddings to funerals. While the legal drinking age in Japan is twenty, when I was growing up it was never enforced at our local convenience store in Minowa, which sold everything from beer, sake, and shochu to bottles of spirits to canned Whisky Highballs.

At age thirteen, I was neither picky nor discerning, but I *was* on a tight budget. I would sneak out at night with my friends on our bikes and ride to the convenience store, which sat on a lonely stretch of highway. In the countryside, the garish lighting of the store made it stand out for miles, signaling a joyous beacon of inebriation. Once inside, we giddily purchased inexpensive shochu and bottom-shelf gins, and made other questionable choices. To make matters worse, we chugged them, which led to a brief and hazy period of drunkenness, followed by throwing up, passing out, and waking up three hours later with massive headaches. Looking back, it was something of a miracle that I didn't suffer from acute alcohol poisoning. If I had to engineer the absolute worst possible introduction to the world of spirits, that would be it, but I still decided to devote my professional life to serving alcohol.

From these decidedly unpromising drinking beginnings in Japan, I have since refined my tastes and moderated my indulgences. In Japan today, there is a mind-boggling array of things to quaff. Three stand out as the most significant, especially for someone devoted to cocktails: sake, shochu, and Japanese whisky. You could write comprehensive books on each of these beverages and, thankfully, others have done so, and very well. But for our purposes, I offer a very brief overview of each and its role in cocktails.

Sake: Japan's Quintessential Pour

Sake is probably the tipple most closely associated with Japan. In fact, sake's proper name is *nihonshu*, which loosely translates to "Japanese hooch." Sake is classified by how much polishing the rice used to brew it has undergone; these classifications include *junmai, honjozo, junmai ginjo, ginjo, junmai daiginjo,* and *daiginjo*. In general, the higher the milling percentage, the more nuanced and subtle the sake. Sake is commonly called rice wine, and from a practical standpoint, it functions similarly to wine. Western sommeliers sometimes serve sake in wineglasses, and its potency, around 14% to 16% ABV, is comparable to the upper reaches of wine, which range between 8% and 14% ABV. But wine is made by fermenting grape juice, while sake is brewed from rice, which technically makes it more akin to beer, a beverage brewed from grain. Moreover, sake is meant to be imbibed fresh like beer, rather than aged like wine (though aged sakes do exist). The similarities stop there—sake traditionally isn't carbonated, doesn't incorporate hops, and has a much higher ABV than beer, which is typically in the 4% to 6% ABV range—so calling sake "rice wine" might not be so dopey after all.

My first memory of trying sake was of my grandfather allowing me to have a sip from his cup. It was easy to drink, with its rice sweetness. But to be frank, when I was living in Japan, I didn't have a true appreciation of sake, which I regarded as a drink for the older generation. I had to learn about it from afar after I moved to New York City. Today, I have embraced sake, both for its ability to pair brilliantly with food and its usefulness as a cocktail ingredient. I am also fascinated by the stories of those who make it. In recent years, sake has been declining in popularity in Japan due to the rise of shochu, whisky, cocktails, wine, beer, and the numerous spirit choices available, but there is an enormous opportunity for sake brands to tell their stories more broadly to capture the imaginations of the next generation of drinkers in Japan and worldwide.

SAKE AND COCKTAILS

As a very delicate ingredient, sake should be treated respectfully. Given its relatively low ABV, I tend to use it not as the base of a cocktail, but as a modifier that adds nuance and flavor to the base spirit. Given the wide flavor and aroma profiles of sake available, it is difficult to generalize, but as a rule, I marry sake with unaged spirits like gin, vodka, and blanco tequila.

At Katana Kitten, the Hinoki Martini is my salute to the sake ritual and a radical reimagining of the Saketini. As in traditional sake service, the cocktail is in a glass that sits inside a square wooden cup known as a *masu*. In this case, it is a stemless martini glass embedded in crushed ice, so the entire drink stays cold until the last sip. For the drink's split base foundation, I marry gin and vodka. In place of vermouth, I use fino sherry and *junmai daiginjo* sake. We also make a punch of Bacardí Carta Blanca rum with a cordial made from *junmai daiginjo* sake and honeydew melon. I also find that this category of sake works beautifully with cucumber in a refreshing Tom Collins variation.

As for my favorite sakes for sipping, that depends entirely on what I am eating, as I seldom sip sake on its own. For cocktails, I love Dassai 50 *junmai daiginjo* for its versatility and aroma. We also serve Yuho, a beautiful *junmai* sake that we incorporate into a pairing with grilled shrimp. The mushroom-like umami notes in the sake amplify those in the dish.

Shochu: Japan's National Spirit

Japan's native and highly popular spirit is shochu, literally meaning "burnt alcohol," referring to the fact that it is distilled. In a very broad sense, if you take sake, a fermented beverage, and distill it, you get shochu. Or, to use a Western analogy, if you distill beer, you get whiskey. However, the comparison to sake ends here, since shochu can be made from countless different grains and other foods, ranging from rice to sweet potatoes, barley to buckwheat, sesame to brown sugar, aloe to chestnuts, and many more, whereas sake is strictly brewed from rice. Shochu is traditionally around 25% ABV, compared with hard spirits that clock in at 40%, making it easy to knock back, especially when further diluted. Its relatively low proof also makes it a very food-friendly spirit.

Traditional shochu is called *honkaku shochu*, and it is single pot distilled. While Western spirits, like vodka, like to boast about how many times they are distilled, each distillation strips away flavor, which, after all, is the point of vodka. In contrast, *honkaku shochu* has a robust flavor, more like a malty genever, unaged whisky, white rum, or even a Polish rye vodka with spicy grain notes, with the

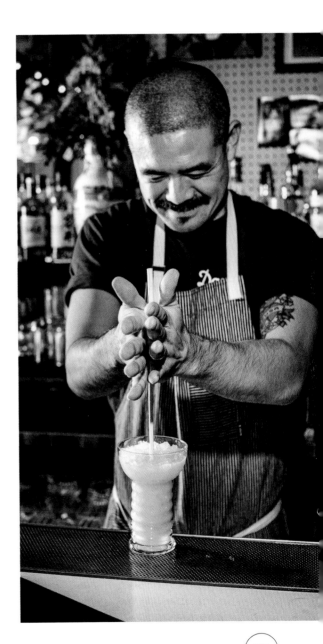

base ingredients really coming through. To my palate, sweet potato shochu is nice and round, whereas shochu made from rice is super light. Buckwheat shochu is toasty and fragrant, with grainy aromas.

SHOCHU AND COCKTAILS

In general, shochu serves as a great base for cocktails that are light-bodied and fruit-, vegetable-, or herb-forward. At Katana Kitten, we use sweet potato shochu and arrack in place of rum in our Mai Tai variation. For sipping, I generally favor sweet potato shochu. For cocktails, I'm enchanted by iichiko Saiten. iichiko is Japan's leading barley shochu producer, and they designed iichiko Saiten specifically for use in cocktails. At 43% ABV, iichiko Saiten is much more potent than traditional *honkaku shochu* and is comparable in proof to vodka, rum, and gin. It has wonderful umami notes that shine through in any drink. Right now, it is only available in the US, but I'm sure that bartenders in Japan will be clamoring for it because of its versatility in cocktails.

Japanese Whisky

When speaking about Japanese whisky, it is hard to generalize. Each house has its own style. Obviously, ingredients are key, and just about everything is imported, from the malted barley to the corn. There just isn't enough available arable land in Japan to grow these crops at volumes necessary for large-scale whisky production. Some producers, like Chichibu, use estate-grown grain, but this is far from the norm. What Japan does have, like Scotland, is massive quantities of top-quality, pure soft water. The four Japanese whisky producers I respect the most are Suntory, Nikka, Chichibu, and Mars Shinshu. This last is in Nagano, about 25 minutes from my parents' home. It produces one of the highest quality Japanese whiskies, a series called Komagatake.

Each whisky house is unique, with a different approach to balancing limited resources, taking advantage of the local climate for aging protocols, as well as their blending philosophy. In contemporary times, the quality of Japanese whisky has, in general, been outstanding, but for many years, it went unnoticed. As an example, in Yamazaki 18, the "18" refers to the age of the *youngest* whisky in the blend. In fact, there is a lot of older spirit, say twenty-five years old, included that gives the whisky an amazing depth of character and layers of flavor.

My first taste of whisky was a canned Whisky Highball in junior high from that now infamous convenience store in Minowa. I remember it tasted weird and a bit sweet. I don't think I liked it at all. Even during my early years of bartending in Japan, we didn't pay too much attention to Japanese whisky, especially compared with today. While we all recognized the quality of the product and carried Yamazaki, Hakushu, and Hibiki, I don't recall guests asking for them that frequently. The best-selling spirits were all imported: Scotch, cognac, and rum. But once Japanese whiskies began winning global awards, this all changed, first in Japan and later in the US. The explosion of interest has driven up demand, but with the long aging regimens, supply has been slow to keep up. Indeed, the very scarcity of some Japanese whiskies makes them even more desirable, comparable to Pappy Van Winkle syndrome in the US.

Overall, I would say that Japanese whisky is perhaps a bit more nuanced and subtle than many others. Many of the whiskies are produced on a relatively small scale. Japan's four distinct seasons nurture the development of the whiskies' flavors and complexity. Moreover, each distillery has a pronounced sense of place. For example, Hakushu is made in an idyllic location, complete with a clear-water creek that is home to prized yamame trout. In the wintertime, the snowy climate is pristine and perfectly quiet. During the summer, the smell of greenery pervades the air. In a sense, when someone buys Hakushu, they are buying that atmosphere.

JAPANESE WHISKY AND COCKTAILS

The archetypal whisky cocktail in Japan is by far the Whisky Highball. It is the rocket engine that propelled whisky back to mainstream popularity in Japan and continues to fuel its growth. Whisky Highballs are ubiquitous across the country and are available in just about every kind of bar and from vending machines. They are reliably well-made

and delicious. The next most popular way is *mizuwari,* which is whisky and water in a 1-to-5 ratio, which dilutes the alcohol level to the point where the drink goes well with food. Finally, enjoying whisky on the rocks is also extremely popular and prevalent throughout Japan.

As a general rule, when using Japanese whisky in cocktails, be certain that the modifiers don't overwhelm the subtle nuances of the spirit, which would defeat the purpose of using it. You want to preserve its flavor. That said, I don't think it is sacrilegious to use pricier Japanese whiskies in mixed drinks and cocktails. It is all about the time, the place, and the occasion.

When it comes to sipping Japanese whisky, I love all the Hibiki expressions. But for cocktails, I'm devoted to Suntory Toki. It is a delicious blended whisky. The corn whisky component comes from the Chita Distillery and gives the whisky a soft, light foundation. Whiskies from Yamazaki and Hakushu add layers of character and complexity. It was designed specifically for use in highballs and cocktails, and it performs spectacularly. At around $40 a bottle US retail, it is eminently affordable for bars to use.

WHAT MAKES A JAPANESE BAR A JAPANESE BAR?

When discussing a Japanese bar, it is important to establish that there are several distinct kinds of drinking destinations, each with its own style, customs, and best drinking choices. If you set your expectations to the appropriate level, you will seldom, if ever, be disappointed, as quality is unfailingly high across the board. Also, there is no culture of tipping in Japan, which definitely applies to its drinking establishments, so keep that in mind for your outings.

There are several basic kinds of bars that you will encounter: mixology-forward cocktail bars, where you can expect classic cocktails expertly prepared and served in luxurious, solemn surroundings; hotel bars, which provide a cocktail bar experience, though in more gregarious settings; izakaya, the country's informal restaurants, where you can carouse with friends; mixology-forward cocktail bars that are on par with the best of the global drinks scene; and *tachinomi* (standing bars), where the drinks are simple and optimized to be sipped on the fly.

Cocktail Bars
WHAT TO EXPECT
Cocktail bars are the pinnacle of Japanese formal mixology. Expect an indulgent experience of perfectly made classic cocktails expertly executed without any unnecessary motion or superfluous ingredients. The bartender is laser-focused on the drink he or she is making in front of them on the bar. It is as if the entire world has come to a standstill, while they prepare that one Manhattan or martini. It is a discrete, uninterrupted experience. The guest sits at the bar and the entire focus is on the guest and the drink. There is a solemnity to the experience that befits the dignity of the art and the craft of the cocktail.

The experience is more in line with attending a performance by an exquisite jazz trio or a solo violinist, not a raging rock concert. The mood is calm and meditative, like Japan's legendary *sado* (Tea Ceremony), never frivolous or flippant. The bartenders view their cocktails as multisensory experiences, and they take their time to make each cocktail a work of art. They work methodically and gracefully, but in an unhurried manner. In many Japanese cocktail bars, especially those in Ginza, there is minimal to no use of speed pours, which are the specialized spouts that bartenders around the world insert into spirits bottles to facilitate a controlled pour. Instead, there is a ritual. The bartender retrieves a bottle from the back bar and places it on the bartop, with the label facing the guest. Holding the bottle with the right hand, the bottle is rotated inward and, using the thumb and middle finger of the left hand, the cap is removed in a single and gracious rapid motion. The bartender now pours using the right hand, while the cap is still held in the left. When the pour is finished, the mouth of the bottle is wiped clean with a towel by the left hand, so that the closure of every bottle, even those containing sticky liqueurs like Chartreuse and Cointreau, is never crystallized with any left-over drips. The bottle is then smoothly recapped and reset on the back bar.

Due to the very limited number of seats, some cocktail bars require reservations. In addition, don't blithely walk in with six of your friends and expect to be accommodated, as the tables are mostly two-tops. Happily, most cocktail bar menus are in Japanese and English, and the bar staff can generally communicate in both.

WHAT YOU'LL BE DRINKING
At cocktail bars, the drinks are faithful renditions of classic cocktails. When you peruse the menu, expect to see many familiar drinks, martinis, daiquiris and Rob Roys. Mind you, Japan never experienced Prohibition, so many of the cocktail recipes have been handed down from sensei to apprentice in an unbroken chain of tradition over a century. So in a way, these bars are living museums, where pre-Prohibition cocktails can be enjoyed more or less the way they were prepared back in the day. Adding to the time-machine appeal, don't be surprised if your cocktail is served in a vintage glass. Take time to admire the exquisite craftsmanship of the cut crystal.

If that weren't enough, if you order the exact same drink again, it will likely be served to you in a completely different vintage glass that is equally stunning.

RULES OF THE ROAD
The main advice I can give first-time cocktail bar visitors is to be respectful and give the bartender your full attention. Please keep your conversation at a quiet level. It's not the place for boisterous laughter or loud banter. This is not the place to get rowdy, and it's important to be respectful of the venue and staff, as well as the other guests at the bar. The best seats are at the bar directly across from the bartender. This is where the performance takes place, and it is a graceful ballet to admire, from the supreme confidence of the well-rehearsed movements to the uncanny economy of motion.

PRICING
The cocktail bar experience comes at a price. In addition to cocktails ranging from $15 to $20, there is often a cover charge of a similar rate tacked onto the bill. In Ginza, the prices reflect the real estate values being among the highest in the world. Most buildings in the area are six stories high, and many bars will aggregate on the upper levels, where the rent is a bit more reasonable.

Hotel Bars
WHAT TO EXPECT
Another kind of bar on the refined end of the spectrum are hotel bars. These bars often offer a cocktail

bar's perfection and refined style of service, and the venues are as beautiful as the drinks themselves. Unlike cocktail bars, however, do not expect a meditative one-on-one experience, as these spots are more social by nature and the bartenders serve multiple guests at once. Hotels have long been on the vanguard of promoting cocktails in Japan, going back to the nineteenth century, and hotel bartenders have their own trade association. They are extremely well trained and take great pride in preparing classic cocktails.

Probably the best-known hotel bar in Tokyo is the New York Bar at the Park Hyatt Tokyo, thanks to it being featured in Sofia Coppola's *Lost in Translation.* Other top spots include the Mandarin Bar at the Mandarin Oriental, Old Imperial Bar at the Imperial Hotel, Maduro at the Grand Hyatt Tokyo at Roppongi Hills, Peter at the Peninsula Hotel, Oak Bar at the Tokyo Station Hotel, and The Bar at the Ritz-Carlton Tokyo.

WHAT YOU'LL BE DRINKING

In the more elegant hotels, as in cocktail bars, it is probably best to stick with classic cocktails. At some of the more modern and hip hotels, creativity is much more the order of the night.

RULES OF THE ROAD

Hotel bars are an excellent introduction for newcomers to Tokyo. Expect solid cocktails and accommodating, well-trained bar teams who can communicate in English.

PRICING

Drinks at hotel bars begin at around $20 and go much higher, depending on the ingredients. As in cocktail bars, there may also be a cover charge, which comes into play when there is live music or if your seats command particularly impressive views.

Izakaya

WHAT TO EXPECT

The next category is izakaya. If you parse out the word, it means a place to live, drink alcohol, and hang out. They are first and foremost restaurants and always serve food, often authentic regional specialties. You'll see izakaya focused on seafood, fried food, grilled skewers—you name it.

WHAT YOU'LL BE DRINKING

On the beverage side, there is typically beer, highballs, shochu, and sake from high-volume dispensers. If the izakaya serves Asahi beer, a sister company of the whisky producer Nikka, do not expect any Suntory whiskies, like Yamazaki, to be served. It is similar to fast-casual US restaurant chains that are either firmly in Coca-Cola's camp or Pepsi's, and never the twain shall meet.

RULES OF THE ROAD

If cocktail bars are formal temples of inebriation, izakaya are where Japanese let their hair down and have a garrulous good time. Enjoy their classic offerings, including beer, highballs and, of course, their food. Izakaya take reservations, and many can accommodate large groups. Often, there is both communal seating and counter seats at the bar, and some even have sidewalk seating. If you're seated inside, don't be surprised if you are asked to take off your shoes and put them in the provided cubby by the door. Don't worry, no one will steal them. There are no uniform hours for izakaya, so do check in advance.

What flabbergasts many visitors to Japan is that there is no "last call." While Tokyo is truly a city that never sleeps, be aware that public transportation does take a long nap between one a.m. and five a.m., and taxi fares can be substantial, potentially equaling a bar tab. Keep an eye on the clock; otherwise, you will have four awkward hours to kill in the bar.

Even in these casual settings, know your limits. Don't fall asleep at the bar, don't pass out, and please, don't throw up on the sidewalk.

PRICING

Easy-on-the-wallet drinks for "one coin," a popular advertising come-on that refers to the 500-yen denomination, the equivalent of $5. And yes, it's a bargain.

Mixology-Forward Cocktail Bars

WHAT TO EXPECT

Another category that I am very excited about is mixology-forward cocktail bars. These bars are often opened by Japanese who were either born abroad or spent considerable time outside the country and have embraced the tenets of contemporary international mixology, with drinks as cutting edge as those you'd find in any global cocktail capital. This includes using seasonal, fresh ingredients, as well as house-made syrups and tinctures, and a more freewheeling and experimental approach to cocktail recipes.

Of particular note is the SG Club by Shingo Gokan, who presided over the bar at Angel's Share in New York City for nearly a decade, and whose career path included being a pastry chef and a pilot before homing in on bartending. His bar was inspired by the first Japanese delegation of the Tokugawa shogunate to visit the US in 1860 and imagines what an American-inspired bar run by these samurai would have been like. It consists of the casual Guzzle on its ground floor and the rarefied Sip downstairs, as well as Savor, a members-only cigar bar upstairs. Shingo is also behind Sober Company, the Odd Couple, and Speak Low, all acclaimed bars in Shanghai.

Bar Trench in Ebisu is co-owned by head bartender Rogerio Igarashi Vaz, a Japanese Brazilian, whose bar offers creative spins, like a Black Manhattan that swaps out vermouth for amaro. It also boasts one of the best absinthe collections in Asia, if you fancy pursuing the green fairy.

At Bar Ben Fiddich, located in Tokyo's Shinjuku district, bartender/owner Hiroyasu Kayama utilizes herbs and spices picked on a farm that has been in his family for over two hundred years. With a humble mortar and pestle, he incorporates them in his spontaneously created cocktails, to astonishing effect. He also conjures his own convincing house versions of vermouth and Campari, often *à la minute*, and absinthe.

43

WHAT YOU'LL BE DRINKING

The drinks at the mixology-forward cocktail bars are incredibly diverse and defy easy generalizations. As a good start, do your homework and find out what the particular bar is famous for and order it. Let the bartender know your drink predilections and preferences, and put your trust in their creativity. You will be richly rewarded.

RULES OF THE ROAD

Depending on the bar, expect a serious, though not solemn, cocktail bar–like atmosphere. Accord the bartender your full attention and respect. As in a cocktail bar, the bartenders will take whatever time is necessary to make your drink perfectly, so patience is definitely a virtue.

PRICING

Expect cocktail bar–like pricing, from $15 to $20 a cocktail.

Tachinomi

WHAT TO EXPECT

The next category is *tachinomi,* or standing bars. As the name implies, there are no seats at these venues—everyone stands. They are usually located near train stations. The trains arrive and leave on the dot, so if you have exactly eight minutes to spare, heading to a *tachinomi* for a quick beer or highball will do the trick quite nicely. Everything here is optimized for speed, so service will be fast and efficient, rather than elaborate.

WHAT YOU'LL BE DRINKING

Whether a beer, a Whisky Highball, or a Shochu Highball, the selection of drinks is incredibly elementary, yet well executed.

RULES OF THE ROAD

Get over your claustrophobia, as you will be standing shoulder to shoulder with strangers.

PRICING

Similar to izakaya, at around "one coin," or $5, a drink.

One of the joys of drinking in Japan, like anywhere, is when you lose your way and happen upon a random place without having any expectations of it. Having a pure experience like this can be a revelation. In the world of cocktails, and most things in life, fortune favors the adventurous. While I admit that getting lost can be a wee bit stressful, confusing, and confounding, it can also be a door to amazing experiences. Moreover, Japanese, by virtue of our culture, are polite and helpful. If they don't speak English, they very well might call a friend who does. So take a chance, leave your hotel, and just get lost. Who knows what you might discover in the process?

JAPANESE BARTENDING STYLES AND TECHNIQUES

Despite the siloing of the various styles of Japanese bartending between mixology-forward cocktail bars, hotel bars, izakaya, and *tachinomi*, there is a commonality that transcends all styles. The most important element is *omotenashi,* the Japanese concept of selfless hospitality. It is about serving guests with one's full heart and subjugating one's ego without putting on airs or being inauthentic. *Omotenashi* deeply pervades Japanese culture, and visitors to the country are always struck by the incredibly high levels of thoughtful service. It doesn't matter if you are in a cocktail bar or a *tachinomi*—the hospitality will be excellent, and the bartender will do his or her utmost to anticipate guests' needs.

Beyond *omotenashi,* there are several bartending styles and techniques that are worth delving into: the Hard Shake, the Art of Ice, and Cocktail Garnishes.

The Hard Shake

Probably the best known, and most misunderstood, of all Japanese bartending techniques is the hard shake, popularized globally by Kazuo Uyeda, the legendary bartender at Tender Bar in Ginza. Some in the bartending community embrace it, while others reject it, saying that any kind of shake, even a randomized one posited by molecular cocktail pioneer and bar owner Dave Arnold, will have similar results in terms of aeration and bringing a drink to proper temperature after twenty to twenty-five shakes. That might all be true, but in my opinion, what sets the hard shake apart is its ability to create an incredibly aerated drink. This texture is quite challenging to achieve, especially in cocktails that do not incorporate egg white.

Despite the name, the object is not to shake the tin so violently that it will shatter the ice within, but rather to have the ice spin inside the shaker to provide the right balance of aeration and agitation. A perfect candidate for the hard shake is the White Lady. Gin, triple sec, and lemon juice get a vigorous shake, yielding a beautiful texture and mouthfeel, composed of tiny bubbles and minuscule shards of ice. The visual opacity is stunning. One of the foremost exemplars of this is Hidetsugu Ueno of Bar High Five, who has made the White Lady his signature drink. The three-piece cobbler shaker, which consists of a cap, a top with a built-in strainer, and a mixing tin, is standard in Japanese bartending, and it is perfectly suited to the technique. If you want to practice the hard shake, it is a good idea to invest in one.

MY HARD SHAKE, REIMAGINED

In the US, we don't see cobbler shakers being widely used professionally, perhaps because two-piece shakers are much easier to clean, especially in high-volume situations. At Katana Kitten, I played around with my own version of the hard shake that achieves unique results. I call it "Fluffy Style."

If I'm making a daiquiri, for example, I'll take a two-piece shaker and pack the larger tin with ice. In the small tin, I add 2 ounces rum, 1 ounce lime juice, and ¾ ounce simple syrup. This mixture goes into a Vitamix I keep behind the bar, and I blend the heck out of it. I'm careful not to blend it too long, as eventually the blender's motor will generate heat, which will "cook" the contents and should be absolutely avoided. The mixture becomes hypersaturated with air bubbles and is then strained into the large tin with the ice, capped with the small tin, and shaken hard. The resulting drink is strained into a frozen glass, and the texture is, well, fluffy. This technique works with any cocktail that doesn't call for egg white, like Sidecars and Gimlets.

Like all Japanese bartending techniques, the hard shake requires discipline and meticulousness. It begins with deliberately selecting the pieces of ice, a combination of cubes and cracked ice that fit together in the shaker like a jigsaw puzzle. Once shaking begins, the question of how long and how hard to shake take a long time to calibrate and perfect and, of course, depend on the specific cocktail being made and the characteristics desired in the finished drink.

When I trained as a bartender in Tokyo, at my bars there was no mention of a specific Japanese shake or the hard shake. We simply learned how to shake properly. What I can say is that the main misconception about the hard shake is that there is a single standard way to do it and everyone does it that way, or at least strives to do so. This is simply not the case. Every bartender does the hard shake in their own way based on their particular musculature and the length of their arms. Some use an overexaggerated motion; others are more fluid. A bartender has to focus on what they are doing and trying to achieve with the particular cocktail and feel the temperature of the shaker in real time. The hard shake demands undivided attention. It has to be a singular endeavor.

The Art of Ice

The other aspect of Japanese bartending that gets a lot of notice, and deservedly so, is the celebration of ice. Elaborate and perfectly clear ice has always been part of Japanese cocktail culture. Nearly every Japanese bar purchases large blocks of ice that they then break down and carve into cubes, spheres, spears, and other shapes. Why not just use an ice machine? First, ice machines are not traditional, so that would not be in keeping with Japanese bartending in cocktail bars and other high-end bartending styles. Second, the machines are large, and the one thing that Japanese bars don't have is space, especially behind the bar. Third, the quality of ice you get from machines just can't compete with the perfection of block ice that is brought in fresh every day.

The epitome of Japanese ice is the legendary ice sphere. Nothing can take the place of an exquisite whisky poured over a perfectly transparent sphere sitting in a rocks glass. Beyond the stunning appearance, the ice sphere's geometry offers practical advantages. By lacking the tapered, pointed edges of a cube, ice spheres do not melt as quickly, thereby preserving the integrity of the spirit by preventing it from being unduly watered down.

So, what is the best way to carve an ice sphere at home? I advise starting with a large block of ice. Since you probably don't have a Clinebell machine, a $15,000 apparatus that makes enviable blocks of transparent ice, I suggest a much cheaper alternative, which was first brought to light by cocktail blogger Camper English. The concept is directional freezing. The first step is to purchase a small Igloo cooler, something that fits a six-pack. Next, remove the lid entirely and set it aside. Fill the cooler with water to a few inches below the top. Place the water-filled cooler in the freezer. Since the cooler has no lid, the water will freeze from top to bottom, pushing any impurities downward. Once frozen, the cooler is taken out of the freezer and inverted, and a clear block of ice emerges. If the bottom part is opaque, this can be carved off with a hand saw. Put the pure block back in the freezer for a few hours to make it hard and tight, then use a hand saw to break the block down into cubes of varying sizes, as well as spears. Alternatively, you can use a soba knife or any 10-inch flat-bladed knife: place the knife on the ice and whack it with a heavy rubber mallet. If you are carving spheres, cut the block into 3-inch cubes.

Place one of the large ice cubes on a clean bar towel and leave it out to temper until it does not have a dry surface. Otherwise, there is a risk of it shattering when cut. Then, place a clean bar towel in your hand as a secure base and place the tempered cube on it. Most folks start with a chisel and begin by carefully chipping off the corners to make a roundish shape. This is then refined into a sphere by using a knife.

In Japan, my mentors taught me to hold an ice pick like I was grasping a pencil. I start by gently picking away at the corners first, constantly rotating the block as I work to ensure the symmetrical sphere. I advise a motion where the palm of your ice pick hand collides with the palm holding the sphere, which will prevent you from stabbing yourself, which is definitely a danger, so be attentive throughout the process. The resulting sphere will look like a pockmarked moon, but you can use an ultra-sharp paring knife to shave off any imperfections. The spheres can be stored in the freezer. During service, they are taken out and allowed to temper until they do not have a dry surface.

Cocktail Garnishes

Cocktail garnishes are another aspect of Japanese bartending that is worth exploring. While garnishes are employed in cocktails around the world to beautify drinks and sometimes to adjust their flavor, many Japanese bartenders invest an incredible amount of time and thought into what some consider an afterthought. They range from simple and purposeful to beautifully ornate. To me, the garnish should make sense and be part of the cocktail. Moreover, it should be edible and nontoxic. I once saw a cocktail garnished with a hydrangea leaf, which is indeed gorgeous, but it's quite poisonous. If you serve something, people assume it's safe to nibble on. Beyond the fruit, vegetable, or spices used to finish a drink, I also consider the serving vessel itself, and even the coaster it's served on, as part of the garnish. In Japan, I have seen cocktails accompanied by a little pastry on the side. This is derived from *sado* (the Tea Ceremony), as the tea is often accompanied by a traditional Japanese sweet, like mochi, or a chocolate confection.

I remember the pleasure of being presented drinks by Japanese bartenders who won a Suntory cocktail competition. The prize was to demonstrate their winning cocktails in New York City. I heard that while most folks on the plane were watching the in-flight movies or trying to sleep, some of the contestants, nattily dressed in suits and ties, were working feverishly, spending hours on the flight creating the most incredibly ornate garnishes anyone had ever seen.

I very well understand their inspiration from studying the art of *ikebana* (also known as *kado*), the Japanese way of arranging flowers that has its roots in ancient times, when flowers were given as offerings in temples and at ancestral shines. *Ikebana* is considered an art form and meditation on par with the Tea Ceremony. While there are many schools and styles of *ikebana,* it is characterized by minimalism, with stems and leaves given equal footing to flowers, and an embrace of the ephemeralness of nature and, by extension, of all life. When applied to cocktails, it can give guests something that is both beautiful and memorable. It is also a way to incorporate seasonality, as specific shapes and motifs can suggest different times of the year.

As you can see, Japanese bartending is complex and multifaceted and its style of service can range from graceful movements and an economy of motion to more straightforward elements of style.

But it is important for bartenders not to fetishize these pursuits and to keep the focus on creating the most delicious cocktails possible. We have to remember what we are doing is serving people to make them happy. They are a means to an end, not the end itself.

KATANA

KITTEN

RECIPES

Now that you know a little bit about the Japanese art of the cocktail and how we brought Katana Kitten to life, it's time to roll up your sleeves and make some drinks. I'm going to show you the ropes of cocktail making, along with some helpful tips and guidance for aspiring home bartenders. With a little practice, you'll be making the same delicious cocktails we make at Katana Kitten in the comfort of your own home. These recipes were honed and refined over many iterations and are a great source of pride for me and our bar team. They are also a handy way for people outside of New York City to experience Katana Kitten without having to make a special trip. But, of course, we do hope to welcome you in person at the bar one day so you can have the full experience. Be sure to say hello.

MAKING KATANA KITTEN DRINKS AT HOME

The following are some helpful guidelines and rules of the road to re-create our recipes at home.

MEASURE TWICE, POUR ONCE

Thoroughly read through all the steps of each recipe before diving in to account for any extra steps or subrecipes you may need to prepare in advance. At Katana Kitten, as in most professional bars, we use a standard jigger to ensure accurate measurements and consistency, and you should, too. Invest in a good set with alternating measurements of 1 ounce/ 2 ounces and ½ ounce/¾ ounce, and you'll have the foundation you need to mix, shake, and stir up these cocktails. Be mindful of the measurements listed in each recipe to achieve the desired balance.

INVEST IN BASIC BAR TOOLS

You don't need every bar tool under the sun, but you will need the core basics to make these drinks. A cocktail shaker set is essential. It can be a pair of metal shakers, the kind preferred by many American craft bartenders, or a combination of a pint glass and a metal top. If you want to practice the hard shake (see page 46), you'll want to consider picking up a three-piece cobbler shaker. There are many ornate barspoons out there, but a basic one with an elongated handle that provides leverage and makes stirring easier will do the trick. You'll need proper cocktail strainers, including a julep strainer, which looks like a perforated dome, for stirred drinks, and a Hawthorne strainer, the flat kind with a coiled spring, for shaken cocktails.

CULTIVATE BRAND AWARENESS

As you will see in the recipes that follow, I note the specific brands of spirits and modifiers used in our cocktails and those contributed by my bartender friends and colleagues. These products vary greatly between producers, and even different expressions of the same spirit from the same maker can be vastly different. As such, I recommend using the brands specified to re-create exactly what we are serving at Katana Kitten and by our contributors at other distinguished bars. In some instances, acceptable substitutes are listed. Of course, if you can't get your hands on a specific bottle, feel free to use a similar spirit. For example, if the recipe calls for a specific rice shochu brand, try another rice shochu. Keep in mind that the drink will likely taste delicious, but it will not be the exact replica of what the bartender had in mind.

ICE, ICE, BABY

You can really go crazy with ice, and in my opinion, having gorgeous, perfectly clear ice is worth the effort. That being said, using ice molds is fine. Be sure to purchase a variety of shapes, including cubes, spears (elongated cubes), and spheres. The resulting ice will be cloudy, but functional. Always use water that has been filtered to remove chlorine, and if your tap water is really questionable, use bottled water. Also make sure there is nothing malodorous in your freezer, as the ice will absorb the off smells. If you have the space and can afford it, having a freezer dedicated to making ice and chilling glasses is a good idea.

For advanced home bartenders, you will want to make your own crystalline blocks of ice that can then be broken down into the desired shape and size. Do this in advance, so you have the specific ice you need on hand when making the drinks. If completely frozen solid, the ice should be tempered until none of its surfaces are dry. Even your refrigerator's ice machine will produce good enough results; just keep in mind that it will melt faster, which affects a drink's dilution.

For crushed ice, purchase a Lewis bag, which is basically a canvas bag, along with a wooden mallet. Place ice cubes in the bag and whack the crap out of them with the mallet. The bag contains the ice and absorbs some of the water created by the tiny shards of ice melting, so it keeps the main ice drier.

GET APPROPRIATE GLASSWARE

At Katana Kitten, our Nick & Nora glasses and cocktail coupes hold 5½ ounces and 7 ounces, respectively, and our shot glasses hold a 1-ounce pour. Our handled beer steins, which we use for highballs, are 12 ounces. It is good practice to keep your glasses and mugs in the freezer, so they will maintain the cocktail's cold temperature when they are pressed into service. Of course, you can always ice down a glass by filling it with water and ice and waiting a few minutes, but who wants to wait?

CREATE SALT RIMS

A salt rim on a glass provides visual appeal and gives a pop of saltiness to your drink. Most folks are acquainted with them from margaritas, and they are easy to execute at home. The first step is to fill a small plate with a mound of salt—at Katana Kitten we use Maldon sea salt—or a specialized seasoning. Then, take a citrus wedge and use it to moisten the rim of the cocktail glass. Some recipes call for a half a rim, in which case you would only moisten half with the citrus wedge. Be sure that the citrus you are using is the same as the citrus in the cocktail. Flip the glass upside down and press the rim into the salt, tilting the glass so the moistened rim comes into contact with the salt, and begin rotating the glass until the rim is coated.

USE FRESH JUICES

Whenever possible, all juices should be freshly squeezed. A wooden citrus reamer is fine for small amounts, but a mechanical lever citrus press or an electric juicer will come in handy if you are making large amounts. The only exception is yuzu juice, since yuzu fruit is very hard to come by in the US, and when you can find it, it is quite expensive. Store-bought imported yuzu juice is quite acceptable. Lastly, there are several recipes that call for "fluffy" juice, the texture of which is quite exceptional. I recommend the Breville 800JEXL Juice Fountain Elite for this purpose.

SIMPLE SYRUP AND NOT-SO-SIMPLE SYRUP

The most basic syrup used in mixology, simple syrup is ridiculously easy to whip up at home, so don't even consider store-bought. All you need is ordinary granulated sugar, the kind that is probably sitting in your pantry right now, and water. The basic recipe is at right.

Stir Up a Storm

Stirring is a basic technique that is critical for mixing the cocktail's ingredients, bringing down its temperature, and diluting the alcohol to a gentler, more drinkable state. It is employed for most drinks that are primarily spirits and imparts a weighty yet silky quality to a cocktail, and a crystalline appearance, like a martini or a Manhattan. If your drink tastes harsh and jagged, it's probably because you didn't stir it long enough. A stirred "up" cocktail will not get further dilution, even though over the course of enjoying the cocktail to the last sip, it will change in temperature, yielding a different mouthfeel and

SIMPLE SYRUP
Makes 2 cups

1¼ cups sugar
1¼ cups water

In a small pot, combine the sugar and water and heat over medium-low heat, stirring frequently to dissolve the sugar completely. Let cool, then pour it into an 1-pint airtight glass container and seal the container. Store in the refrigerator for up to 1 month.

NOTE: *In a pinch, you can use room-temperature water, but you will have to agitate it vigorously to dissolve the sugar and the process will take longer compared to the heated method. A Vitamix or similar heavy-duty blender can expedite the process.*

RICH SIMPLE SYRUP: *Follow the same instructions but use 2 parts sugar to 1 part water.*

DEMERARA SYRUP: *Swap in Demerara sugar for the regular sugar (Demerara syrup provides a fuller, richer flavor compared to simple syrup).*

FLAVORED SIMPLE SYRUPS: *Simply add a flavoring ingredient to the basic mix, such as lime zest or vanilla beans, to create lime simple syrup or vanilla simple syrup, respectively. Generally, the flavoring ingredient is added during the heating process to speed up the infusion and is then strained out. These syrups also come in handy for iced coffee or iced tea, since sugar is difficult to dissolve in cold liquids.*

flavor. Stirred drinks served on the rocks do experience further dilution. It would be nice if I could say, "Stir your cocktail a certain number of times clockwise and a specific number of times counterclockwise," but every drink is different, and stirring is a skill that you will acquire over time with practice. It will all depend on the temperature and type of the ice, the mixing vessel's size and material, and the ambient room temperature.

STIRRING HIGHBALLS

Everything we do when it comes to our highballs is to preserve the carbonation. Stirring rigorously will liberate the CO_2 and result in losing precious bubbles. Instead, we want to incorporate as little kinetic energy as possible into the motion. One technique that I find effective is to insert a barspoon into the bottom of the drink and gently lift and lower the ice a few times. This, plus a slow, gentle stir, mixes the ingredients with the least amount of agitation.

Shake It Up

This technique is used whenever a cocktail calls for fresh juices, eggs, syrups, or opaque liqueurs, which are difficult to combine by just stirring. In addition to the benefits we saw with stirring, shaking also brings aeration to the mix. It makes your Gimlet lively, thanks to the tiny air bubbles incorporated. Shaking should be done with a rapid repetitive motion. Rather than a simple back-and-forth piston action, which shatters the ice within the shaker and overdilutes the drink, a circular motion should be introduced

so that the ice is revolving intact within the shaker, thereby mixing and aerating the contents. As with stirring, there is no set formula for shaking—I can't say, "Shake every drink for 15 seconds." You will get a feel for it over time, so that after shaking your drinks are not over- or underdiluted, and are at the proper temperature and texture.

How Dry I Am

Some of the recipes here call for dehydrating specific ingredients, which removes moisture and concentrates their flavor. If you have a dehydrator at home, you're in luck—simply follow the manufacturer's directions. If you don't, just use your oven on its lowest setting. Keep an eye on whatever you're dehydrating and test samples to determine if it is sufficiently dehydrated. Store your dehydrated ingredients in an airtight glass container; otherwise, they will absorb ambient moisture from the air and will be less crisp.

Tiny Bubbles

Having a home carbonation system means you never have to worry about running out of sparkling water, and there are also several ingredients in this book that require being carbonated. At Katana Kitten, we use a simple 20-pound CO_2 tank attached to a regulator and ball-lock carbonator; the method is force carbonation, popularized by molecular mixology pioneer Dave Arnold. SodaStream and iSi offer home consumer–friendly options. Be sure to follow the manufacturer's instructions.

57

Top It Off

Many recipes in this book call for topping with chilled soda water. This means that the cocktail is built in the glass with the ice and various ingredients are added in succession. Then plain soda or seltzer is poured in until it reaches the top of the cocktail glass. Other "toppings" can include Champagne, beer, and bubbly soft drinks. The actual amount to be poured will depend on the size and shape of the glass and the amount of ice occupying it.

Float Away

Sometimes, you want the final ingredient of a cocktail to sit at the top of the drink rather than be mixed in. This provides a color contrast and sometimes distinctive aromatics and is a great way to spotlight that particular ingredient. To execute a float, simply place a spoon on the top of the cocktail, domed-side up. Then, slowly and gently, pour the ingredient onto the back of the spoon so it flows down onto the cocktail. Remove the spoon, and the ingredient will remain at the top of the cocktail glass.

Fresh and Pretty Garnishes

Garnishes are something of a badge of pride for all bartenders, little works of art that say, "This drink is complete." It is really its own admirable art form. From my perspective, simple garnishes do the trick. Invest in a good paring knife for slicing citrus wedges, wheels, and twists. A Kuhn Rikon Origin Swiss peeler makes short work of preparing the latter, which should be done to order, as they dry out quickly.

Making Syrups and Cordials

In the recipes calling for the zests of citrus fruits (lime, lemon, orange, grapefruit, yuzu, etc.), use the Kuhn Rikon peeler noted above to remove a strip of the colorful skin of the fruit and try to take off a minimal amount of the white pith below it, as the pith is quite bitter. Do not be tempted to use a zester or a Microplane rasp grater, as intact strips of zest are much easier to work with.

1

HIGHBALLS

AT KATANA KITTEN, WE'RE KNOWN FOR OUR HIGHBALLS.
Theoretically uncomplicated, their very simplicity dictates
that they be properly made, or they will be disappointing. It
is all about the temperature, ice, and carbonation—each matters. At Katana Kitten, highballs are served as they should
be: supremely icy cold, so that the last bubbly sip is just
as frigid and effervescent as the first. The service vessel that I chose is a 12-ounce glass beer stein with a handle.
Holding the glass by the handle keeps warm fingers away from
the glass itself and better preserves the cold temperature
of the drink. This mug is typically used in casual izakaya or
tachinomi in Japan, where they are also used for beer. The
surprise at Katana Kitten is that the mug is straight from the
freezer, so it is frigid through and through. We source our
ice from Okamoto Studio in New York City, which is renowned for
breathtaking ice sculptures by Shintaro Okamoto, a second-
generation ice maker and ice artist. The company also sup-
plies top cocktail bars with crystalline ice blocks, so our
ice is absolutely pure and dead clear, almost to the point
where you can't see it in the cocktail. Strictly speaking, a
highball is simply a combination of spirits and a sparkling
mixer, for example, whiskey and ginger, gin and tonic, rum
and Coke, or even vodka and Red Bull. But as you will see, at
Katana Kitten, we allow ourselves a few liberties and embel-
lishments, while staying true to the drink's spirit.

TOKI HIGHBALL

In addition to our original highballs, our Toki Highball has been a remarkable success, and we sell more of them than any other bar in the world, according to Suntory, which produces the drink's namesake Toki Whisky. While you can't make Katana Kitten's high-tech Toki Highball without a specialized machine, I will share techniques for making a good approximation at home. But the machine itself is worth knowing about. It was first brought to my attention by Gardner Dunn, Suntory's US brand ambassador and a longtime friend and colleague who has a deep reverence for Japanese drinking culture. He gave me a heads-up that Suntory, one of Japan's premier spirits producers, was pioneering a game-changing device in a partnership with Hoshizaki, which makes some of the country's best ice machines. The machine provides one of the highest levels of carbonation that have ever been experienced, and blows the bubbles in conventional soda and even Champagne out of the water. This pressurization creates a cascade of powerful bubbles that is optimal for conveying flavor. But temperature is equally important, as CO_2 only stays dissolved best in very cold liquids. Open a room-temperature bottle of Coke or sparkling wine, and you'll see exactly what I mean. Better yet, don't. The machine uses a proprietary circulating water bath to keep both the highly carbonated soda and the Toki Whisky itself at barely above freezing to maximize the carbonation and dispense the coldest and bubbliest drink possible at around 37°F.

The machine's whisky-to-soda ratio is customizable and proprietary per each bar. At Katana Kitten, we set the ratio so that it is slightly boozier compared with highballs commonly served in Japan, which reflects the preference of our clientele. The machine's dispenser is also versatile and acts like a stick shift on a sleek sports car. If you hit the dispenser straight on, you get a perfect Toki Highball. If you push it to the right and pull, out comes hypercarbonated water that we use to top off our other highballs. Push to the left and pull, you get frigid Toki Whisky. And if you have never tried a nearly frozen Toki Whisky shot, it is viscous and delicious. The machine's water filters are supposed to last six months, but due to our exceptional

volume, we replace them every two months. Katana Kitten burned through 120 cases of Toki Whisky in a record five months from when we first opened. Served in our frigid glass mugs with perfectly clear ice spears, it is bubbly, refreshing, and utterly satisfying. The garnish is expressed lemon oil and a single ume (Japanese plum).

Unless you own a bar and have close to $5,000 to spend, you probably won't have access to your very own Toki Highball machine. But all is not lost. Simply get your hands on excellent highly carbonated bottled soda water. Purchase the smallest bottles or cans possible, as the large containers lose their carbonation rapidly after they're opened. Keep them as cold as possible prior to use.

With a bottle of Suntory Toki Whisky (I suggest keeping it in the freezer), an icy-cold highly carbonated bottle of soda water, a highball glass, and ice, you are ready to prepare your very own Toki Highball. Make sure your barspoon is not warm from the dishwasher—any kind of heat is the enemy of carbonation and should be eliminated throughout the process.

Here is my method for a perfect one: Take the highball glass and fill it with ice. If the glass has been stored in the freezer, you are all set. If not, simply stir the ice around to sufficiently chill the glass, then strain out any water. Now the fun part. Gently pour a jigger's worth of Suntory Toki Whisky into the glass and stir lightly, adding more ice, if necessary. Slowly and deliberately pour chilled soda water into the glass, aiming for the glass's side wall, not the ice itself, since the shock of the impact with the ice will dissipate the soda water's carbonation. Then, using a stirrer, gently lift the ice up and down a couple of times to mix the whisky and soda water, and give it a slow, gentle stir. A citrus twist garnish is optional, with lemons, limes, yuzu, or other citrus fruits all popular.

In addition to whisky on the rocks, the next most prevalent serve is *mizuwari,* whisky and plain water at a ratio of about 1 to 5. The method of preparation is identical to the Whisky Highball, except chilled water is used instead of soda and there is no garnish. Both *mizuwari* and highballs are exceptionally food-friendly.

AKI PALOMA

SERVES

ONE

With *aki* meaning "autumn," this highball is a celebration of all things fall, and a popular seasonal serve at Katana Kitten. In Japan, during the cooler months, *hojicha,* or roasted green tea, is very popular. It is produced by toasting dried green tea leaves in porcelain pans over charcoal fires. This imparts a faintly warm, toasty flavor. The aroma, for me, conjures up the same feeling people get when they smell a pile of raked leaves burning on a fall afternoon. It is the essence of the season. In this cocktail, I use toasted jasmine tea to evoke the same sense memory. To provide a citrus kick, I use pomelo, which is an enormous grapefruit-like fruit. Its zest is very aromatic, so we incorporate it in a syrup. The flesh is rather dry and doesn't produce a lot of juice when squeezed, so we dehydrate it and blended it with salt to use as a tasty garnish.

1½ ounces Olmeca Altos Plata tequila

¾ ounce ruby grapefruit juice

¼ ounce yuzu juice

¾ ounce Toasted Jasmine–Pomelo Syrup (recipe follows)

Soda water, chilled

Garnish: Smoked Pomelo Salt (recipe follows)

Combine the tequila, grapefruit juice, yuzu juice, and syrup in a highball glass with an ice spear or a stack of ice cubes. Stir gently and top with chilled soda water. Garnish with smoked pomelo salt.

TOASTED JASMINE–POMELO SYRUP

Makes 3¼ cups

Zest of ¼ pomelo, cut into strips with a peeler or paring knife

2 cups sugar

3 tablespoons loose jasmine tea leaves

2 cups water

In a small bowl, muddle the pomelo zest with the sugar to combine and let stand for 30 minutes. In a medium saucepan, gently toast the jasmine tea leaves over medium-low heat, moving the pan constantly, for about 4 minutes. Turn off the heat and let cool. In a small pot, combine the water, zest-sugar mixture, and toasted tea leaves. Bring the mixture to a simmer over medium heat and stir to dissolve the sugar. Remove from the heat and let cool, then strain through cheesecloth into an airtight glass container. Seal the container and store in the refrigerator for up to 1 month.

SMOKED POMELO SALT

Makes 1 cup

1 pomelo
¼ cup smoked Maldon sea salt
¼ cup Maldon sea salt

Dehydrate the pomelo flesh in a dehydrator following the manufacturer's instructions. (It should result in ½ cup of dried pomelo flesh.) Combine the dehydrated pomelo with the salts in an airtight 1-cup glass container. Seal the container and store in the pantry for up to 1 year.

BRIGHT 'N' SUNNY

SERVES

ONE

My take on the classic Dark 'n' Stormy gets a colorful twist courtesy of a splash of rum infused with butterfly pea flower, a Southeast Asian plant commonly used for beverages and desserts, and the source of the drink's distinctive blue hue. Beyond rum, the cocktail incorporates tepache, a fermented beverage popular in Mexico, typically made with pineapple skins, cinnamon, and piloncillo, an unrefined natural cane sugar popular throughout Latin America. The first time I saw a jar of tepache was when one of our bar backs left a batch of it in the walk-in cooler at Saxon + Parole. Due to its funky and suspicious look, I almost tossed it. But thankfully, I came around to appreciating it. Our house version uses the traditional pineapple skins and gives it an Asian twist with lemongrass and ginger, which salutes the Dark 'n' Stormy's ginger beer.

5 ounces Ginger-Lemongrass Tepache (recipe follows)

½ ounce fresh lime juice

1¾ ounces Butterfly Pea Flower Tea-Infused Banks 5 Island Rum (recipe follows)

Garnish: dehydrated pineapple wheel

Place an ice spear or a stack of ice cubes in a frozen highball stein, then add the tepache and lime juice. Using the back of a barspoon, float the rum on top to create a vibrant purple layer as the top third of the drink. Garnish with a dehydrated pineapple wheel.

GINGER-LEMONGRASS TEPACHE

Makes 5½ cups

¾ cup sugar

4 cups water

Skin of ½ pineapple, cut into strips with a paring knife

1 cup finely chopped fresh ginger

2 lemongrass stalks, dry outer husks removed, finely chopped

⅛ teaspoon Champagne yeast (available at homebrewing and winemaking stores or online)

In a large container, dissolve the sugar in the water. Add the pineapple skin, ginger, lemongrass, and yeast and cover the top of the container with cheesecloth so that the mixture can "breathe." Set aside at room temperature (or at about 65°F) for 24 hours until the mixture has a funky yet tropical pineapple aroma. Transfer to a large stockpot. Bring the mixture to 185°F over medium heat and simmer for 5 minutes. Strain through cheesecloth into a 1-liter glass bottle and chill completely. Carbonate using an iSi Soda Syphon or other home carbonation system. Store in the bottle in the refrigerator for up to 1 week.

BUTTERFLY PEA FLOWER TEA–INFUSED BANKS 5 ISLAND RUM

Makes 750ml

1 (750ml) bottle Banks 5 Island rum

1½ teaspoons butterfly pea flower tea leaves

Combine the rum and tea in an airtight 1½-pint glass container and infuse for 2 hours. Strain through cheesecloth into the original rum bottle. Store at room temperature for up to 1 year.

MELON-LIME SODA

SERVES

ONE

I have lived in New York City for more than a decade, and during this time I have made countless vodka-sodas with lime for guests. The Melon-Lime Soda is my Japanese-accented salute to this simple yet extremely ubiquitous drink. This drink is super-refreshing and a carefully balanced layers of all things green. Its vibrant green hue comes from Midori reinforced by matcha. Midori, popular here during the Days of Disco, is an emerald-colored, muskmelon flavored liqueur. Absolut Lime vodka, a housemade matcha-lime cordial, and a blend of the juice of limes and sudachi, a Japanese citrus fruit with a zesty, sour tang, make for a uniquely tart sipping experience. Interestingly, Midori has an intimate connection to *Saturday Night Fever*, the film that helped usher in the aforementioned glittery era and catapulted John Travolta to movie stardom. The movie premiered in Manhattan, and the afterparty was held at Ian Schrager's legendary Studio 54, where, earlier that evening, Midori was introduced to the US for the very first time. Come to think of it, maybe I should have called the drink "Stayin' Alive"!

1 ounce Absolut Lime vodka

1 ounce Midori

½ ounce Matcha-Lime Cordial (recipe at right)

¼ ounce sudachi juice

¼ ounce fresh lime juice

Soda water, chilled

Garnish: fresh lime leaf

Place an ice spear or a stack of ice cubes in a frozen highball stein. Add the vodka, Midori, matcha-lime cordial, sudachi juice, and lime juice. Top off with chilled soda water and gently stir. Garnish with a lime leaf.

MATCHA-LIME CORDIAL

Makes 2 cups

1¼ cups sugar

1¼ cups hot water

Zests of 4 limes, cut into strips with a peeler or paring knife

2½ teaspoons matcha green tea powder

Set aside 3 tablespoons of the water. Combine the sugar and remaining water in a saucepan and heat over low heat to just below a simmer, stirring constantly. Once all the sugar has dissolved and right before the simmering, remove from the heat, add the lime zest, cover the saucepan, and let cool to room temperature; the edges of the lime zest should be lightly browned. Strain the syrup through cheesecloth into an airtight 1-pint glass container.

In a small bowl, whisk the matcha powder in the reserved 3 tablespoons water until fully combined. Add the matcha solution to the syrup and stir well to combine. Seal the container and store in the refrigerator for up to 1 month. Shake the syrup well prior to using, as the matcha has a tendency to settle on the bottom.

RINGO COLLINS

SERVES

ONE

While I love the Beatles, the word *ringo* here refers to the Japanese word for "apple." Apples grow throughout much of Japan, including in my home prefecture, Nagano, where Fuji apples are particularly prized. So, for this Collins variation at Katana Kitten, I wanted to harness the fruit's incredible aromatic properties. I chose a base of California brandy infused with Earl Grey tea. The tea's bergamot citrus notes really bring out the sweet aromatics of the apple. A bit of sherry and umeshu, Japan's iconic plum liqueur, lengthen and lighten the drink. Since we juice our own apples to make our Fuji Apple–Maple Sherbet, we take the leftover pulp and turn it into fruit leather that we then cut into a maple leaf shape for the drink's garnish.

1 ounce Earl Grey Tea-Infused Brandy (recipe follows)

¾ ounce dry umeshu

¾ ounce Manzanilla sherry

¾ ounce Fuji Apple–Maple Sherbet (recipe follows)

Soda water, chilled

Garnish: maple leaf-shaped piece of Fruit Leather (recipe follows) and grated nutmeg

Place an ice spear or a stack of ice cubes in a frozen highball stein. Add the brandy, umeshu, sherry, and sherbet. Stir gently and top with chilled soda water. Garnish with a maple leaf–shaped piece of fruit leather and grated nutmeg.

EARL GREY TEA-INFUSED BERTOUX BRANDY

Makes 750ml

1 (750ml) bottle Bertoux Brandy

1 tablespoon loose Earl Grey tea leaves

Combine the brandy and tea leaves in an airtight 1-quart glass container. Steep for 4 hours at room temperature. Strain into the brandy original bottle. Store in the pantry for up to 1 year.

FUJI APPLE–MAPLE SHERBET

Makes 2 cups

Zests of 3 lemons, cut into strips with a peeler or paring knife

1 cup granulated sugar

¼ cup maple sugar

1 cup cold-pressed Fuji apple juice

¼ cup yuzu juice

¼ cup fresh lemon juice

½ teaspoon citric acid

In a medium bowl, muddle the lemon zest with the granulated sugar and maple sugar. Add the apple juice, yuzu juice, lemon juice, and citric acid and stir to dissolve the sugars. Fine-strain into an airtight 1-pint glass container. Seal the container. Store in the refrigerator for up to 2 weeks.

FRUIT LEATHER

Makes 2 cups

10 cups diced peeled apples (½-inch dice), plus the leftover pulp from making sherbet, if desired

8½ cups water

4½ cups sugar

In a large saucepan, combine the apples, water, and sugar and cook over medium-low heat until the apples have softened. Strain the apples, reserving the liquid, and transfer them to a heavy-duty blender. Puree until smooth, adding some of the reserved liquid, if necessary. Spread the puree in a ⅛-inch-thick layer on a baking sheet and dehydrate until it dries completely. Cut into shapes, if desired, and place in an airtight 1-pint glass container. Store in the freezer for up to 6 months.

SHISO-QUININE CORDIAL

Makes 2 cups

Zest of 3 limes, using a peeler

1½ cups sugar

20 fresh shiso leaves

1½ cups water

¼ ounce organic quinine concentrate

¼ teaspoon malic acid

In a medium bowl, muddle the lime zests with the sugar. Cover and let stand for 30 minutes. Add the shiso leaves and muddle, then cover and let stand for 30 minutes more. Add the water, quinine, and malic acid and stir until all the sugar has dissolved. Strain through cheesecloth into an airtight 1-pint glass container. Seal the container and store in the refrigerator for up to 1 month.

This highball is one of our top sellers, and we use it to highlight the flavor of shiso, a fragrant Japanese leaf that I grow in a community garden in Brooklyn. The gin I use here is Fords gin, created by eighth-generation distiller Charles Maxwell of Thames Distillery, together with Simon Ford, a beloved figure in the bar world. Its juniper-forward profile and citrusy and floral notes make a great base for my take on a classic gin and tonic. It's spiked with an aromatic cordial with a bitter backbone that's invigorated by shiso, an herb that marries the fragrant qualities of mint and basil. Unlike most cordials or syrups that are heated and essentially "cook" their flavoring ingredients, this one is prepared at room temperature to ensure that the pure, vibrant flavor of fresh shiso comes shining through.

1½ ounces Fords gin (or your favorite London dry-style gin)

¾ ounce Shiso-Quinine Cordial (recipe at left)

⅓ ounce fresh lime juice

Soda water, chilled

Garnish: shiso leaf

Place an ice spear or a stack of ice cubes in a frozen highball stein. Add the gin, cordial, and lime juice to the glass, top with chilled soda water, and gently stir. Garnish with a shiso leaf.

SHISO GIN & TONIC

SERVES

ONE

HIGHBALLS

YUZU SPRITZ

The Yuzu Spritz is one of the most quaffable highballs at Katana Kitten. It is both easy to drink and delightfully refreshing. Umeshu is a fruity, sweet, and fragrant Japanese liqueur made from unripe green ume (plums) and a white spirit or shochu. It's often made at home, with families passing down their own recipes from generation to generation. In this cocktail, it's a great companion to the delicate Manzanilla sherry and the gentian-based French liqueur Salers. An added dash of salinity comes with *asazuke* (quick-pickled) cucumbers.

1 ounce Choya umeshu (Japan's most popular brand, which is widely distributed in the US)

1 ounce Manzanilla sherry

½ ounce Salers Apéritif

¾ ounce Yuzu-Lemon Sherbet Syrup (recipe follows)

Soda water, chilled

Garnish: 3 slices of Cucumber Asazuke (recipe follows) on a skewer

Place an ice spear or a stack of ice cubes in a frozen highball stein. Add the umeshu, sherry, Salers, and sherbet syrup. Top off with chilled soda water and stir gently. Garnish with 3 slices of cucumber asazuke on a skewer.

SERVES

ONE

YUZU-LEMON SHERBET SYRUP
Makes 2 cups

Zest of 3 lemons, using a peeler

1¼ cups sugar

1 cup fresh lemon juice

¼ cup yuzu juice

In a medium bowl, muddle the lemon zests with the sugar. Add the lemon juice and yuzu juice and stir to dissolve the sugar. Strain through cheesecloth into an airtight 1-pint glass container. Seal the container and store in the refrigerator for up to 2 weeks.

CUCUMBER ASAZUKE
Makes 1½ cups

6 Persian cucumbers, cut into ¼-inch-thick slices

1½ teaspoons salt

1 small (1-inch-wide) piece kombu (dried Japanese kelp)

1 (1-inch-wide) strip of lemon zest

½ ounce yuzu juice

Combine all the ingredients in an airtight 1-pint glass container or a 1-pint resealable plastic bag. Seal the container or bag and shake to mix everything well and ensure that the cucumbers are well-coated with the brine. Let stand for 5 minutes, drain all the liquid from the container or bag. Seal again and store the cucumbers in the refrigerator for up to 1 day.

2

COCKTAILS

THE SIGNATURE COCKTAILS AT KATANA KITTEN ARE OUR unique takes on iconic drinks that need no explanation. Each of them starts with a classic cocktail recipe that we tweak to make it our own with an eye to the changing seasons. To transform them into Katana Kitten cocktails, we incorporate pops of Japanese flavors and traditions. The drinks are easily recognizable but contain wonderful surprises that our guests adore.

This cocktail is my take on a well-made saketini, and it is very special to me. Over the years, I have been asked numerous times to make this drink, which is basically a vodka martini with sake substituted for the dry vermouth. The sake typically makes the drink a bit sweeter and rounder. For our rendition, I wanted to create a cocktail that honored the Japanese traditional sake serve and the classic dry martini. Hinoki is the Japanese cypress that is used to make the *masu,* the wooden cup used to serve sake. When sake is poured into a *masu,* the scent of cypress becomes part of the experience. To re-create this sensation, I had to source the essence of *hinoki,* which did not exist. We solved this by creating our own. Unfortunately, you can't exactly re-create this cocktail as I make it at Katana Kitten without a few drops of a key ingredient, a cypress tree distillate, but I've provided a handy workaround to create an approximation.

The presentation of the drink is inspired by the traditional sake serve, where a glass is placed in a *masu* and filled until it overflows into the *masu,* a sign of expansive generosity. We serve the drink in a custom wooden *masu* created for us by Cocktail Kingdom. The *masu* is filled with crushed ice, so the entire surface of the stemless cocktail glass containing the drink has contact with the ice to keep it absolutely cold to the very last sip.

To obtain the cypress aroma, I collaborated with Jeff Lindauer, a good friend of mine from Spring44 Distilling in Colorado. We went up into the Rocky Mountains where cypress trees grow in abundance. We identified a varietal that is closest to Japanese cypress, chopped it down, and extracted cypress oil. We first tried a maceration, but it didn't quite capture the flavor, so we fired up the still and created a 140-proof distillate. The unique and irreplaceable flavor of the tree is captured in the bottle. In this recipe, I provide the closest approximation, which is a homemade *hinoki* tincture. If you can't source *hinoki* wood chips, experiment with other types of wood or omit the tincture completely. You will still have a delightfully dry martini to enjoy.

RECIPE CONTINUES

HINOKI MARTINI

SERVES

ONE

COCKTAILS

1¼ ounces Grey Goose vodka

1¼ ounces Spring44 Mountain Gin

½ ounce Lustau "Solera Reserva" fino jarana sherry

¼ ounce Dassai 50 junmai daiginjo sake

5 dashes Hinoki Tincture (recipe follows)

Garnish: lemon twist, kombu-brined olive, rakkyo (pickled Japanese scallion bulb), and cypress leaf

Fill a square wooden masu cup with pebble ice and place a chilled stemless martini glass in the ice. Combine the vodka, gin, sherry, sake, and hinoki tincture in a mixing glass filled with ice. Stir until chilled and strain into the glass. Express a lemon twist over the surface of the drink and discard, then spray four bursts of hinoki tincture over the drink. Delicately adorn the pebble ice around the glass with a kombu-brined olive, rakkyo, and a cypress leaf.

HINOKI TINCTURE
Make 2 cups

½ cup hinoki wood chips
2 cups Everclear or high-proof vodka

Combine the wood chips and Everclear in an airtight 1½-pint glass container and allow the chips to macerate for 24 hours. Strain into an airtight 1-pint container glass. Divide some of the tincture into a 4-ounce atomizer bottle and a 4-ounce dropper bottle, storing the remainder in the glass container. Seal the containers and store in the pantry indefinitely.

SALTED PLUM SHRUB
Makes 2 cups

5 pieces soft umeboshi
(pickled Japanese plums)

1¼ cups water

1 cup sugar

½ cup clover honey

¼ cup Champagne vinegar

In a small saucepan, combine the umeboshi and water and heat gently to a simmer, stirring continuously with a whisk to break down the umeboshi. Turn off the heat, then add the sugar, honey, and vinegar and stir to dissolve the sugar. Cover and let cool. Strain through cheesecloth into an airtight 1-pint glass container, twisting the cheesecloth to extract all the liquid. Seal the container and store in the refrigerator for up to 1 month.

This is my homage to Portland, Oregon, bartender and author Jeffrey Morgenthaler, who created an improved version of the 1970s-era amaretto sour by cutting its treacly namesake liqueur with a high-proof American whiskey to dry it out. Our riff gets an added kick from a high-proof rye, but our special Katana Kitten touch is the addition of a Salted Plum Shrub, which provides a lingering umami taste and a unique salinity. Despite its subtle flavor, this drink hits all the senses, and that's why people order it again and again. The final touch is *yukari,* a Japanese seasoning made from salted and dried red shiso leaves.

1¼ ounce Wild Turkey 101 rye

¾ ounce Lazzaroni amaretto

¾ ounce Salted Plum Shrub
(recipe at left)

¾ ounce fresh lemon juice

¾ ounce egg white

Garnish: Lemon twist and a sprinkle of yukari (salted and dried red shiso)

Combine the rye, amaretto, shrub, lemon juice, and egg white in a cocktail shaker and dry shake without ice to emulsify the egg white. Add ice and shake until chilled. Strain into a double old-fashioned glass over a 2-inch ice cube. Express a lemon twist over the drink and discard, then garnish with a sprinkle of yukari.

AMARETTO SOUR

SERVES

ONE

COCKTAILS

85

MEGURONI

The classic Negroni has inspired
countless variations, and Katana
Kitten's is named after Meguro, the
Tokyo neighborhood nearby where I
used to live. The banks of the Meguro
River are lined with thousands of
sakura (cherry blossom) trees,
and when the blossoms are in
season, locals head over to take in
the gorgeous views. In this drink,
I swap out the traditional gin
for genever, since its round and
malty flavors work best with the
drink's other ingredients. Instead
of vermouth, we use a full-bodied
umeshu (plum liqueur) that has a
color akin to sweet vermouth and a
similar sweetness level, yet tastes
completely different and totally
transforms the drink. The umeshu's
base is actually Japanese blackstrap
rum. Lastly, instead of the traditional
Campari, we opt for an aperitivo
liqueur made with bitter Calabrian
oranges. The final touch is a garnish
of fresh *kinome* leaves.

1 ounce Old Duff Dutch genever

¾ ounce Choya Kokuto umeshu

¾ ounce Caffo Red Bitter

Garnish: lemon twist and fresh
kinome leaves

Combine the genever, umeshu, and
Caffo Red Bitter in a mixing glass
filled with ice. Stir until chilled and
strain into a double old-fashioned
glass or teacup over ice. Express
a lemon twist over the drink and
discard, and garnish with fresh
kinome leaves.

COCKTAILS

SERVES

ONE

CREATING THE RIGHT VESSEL FOR THE RIGHT DRINK

At Katana Kitten, we serve the Meguroni in a custom ceramic cup made for us by my friend Ritsuko Moore. A while back, my former boss, Yoshihiro Shinkawa, and his wife, Mami, visited me in New York City. We went to PDT (Please Don't Tell), the renowned East Village cocktail destination, to get drinks and catch up. Mami brought a close friend, Ritsuko. The two had worked together as flight attendants back in the day. Ritsuko now devotes herself entirely to ceramics and creates bespoke plates for many of New York City's restaurants. Her ceramics are exquisite works of art and embody *wabi-sabi,* the very Japanese concept that venerates the beauty of imperfect, transient objects. Ritsuko is a one-woman operation, and I asked her if she could make cups for us at Katana Kitten. To my surprise and delight, she agreed.

We created a prototype with the outside of the cup the natural raw color of sand and the inside enameled pure white to stand out in the bar. We also calculated how the cup should open up and the amount of headspace above the washline. After many trials, we got it right, and the cups are now an integral part of the experience.

SHIO KOJI PANDAN SYRUP

Makes 2 cups

1¼ cups water

1¼ cups sugar

2 whole pandan leaves

½ ounce shio koji
(available at Japanese
markets and online)

In a small saucepan,
combine the water and
sugar and heat over
medium heat, stirring to
dissolve the sugar. Add the
pandan leaves and bring
the mixture to a simmer.
Remove from the heat,
cover, and let cool. Strain
through cheesecloth, add
the shio koji, and blend
in a heavy-duty blender.
Transfer to an airtight
1-pint glass container.
Seal the container and
store in the refrigerator
for up to 1 month.

The base of this Katana Kitten
take on a daiquiri highlights a
Japanese rum, Cor Cor. The rum
is produced on the small, remote
island of Minamidaito in Okinawa
Prefecture. Cor Cor cultivates their
own sugarcane on their estate and
produces two expressions, one from
sugarcane juice in the style of a rhum
agricole and one from molasses,
which we use in this cocktail. It
is a very unique and pungent rum
that has a lot of earthy notes you
would expect from a Jamaican
rum or a Haitian clairin, which
we balance with a dry Barbados
rum. To complement the lime and
yuzu juices, we make a syrup that
combines *shio koji,* a Japanese
condiment made of salt, water and
rice koji, and pandan leaves.

1½ ounces Mount Gay silver rum

½ ounce Cor Cor Red Okinawan rum

¾ ounce Shio Koji Pandan Syrup
(recipe at left)

½ ounce fresh lime juice

¼ ounce yuzu juice

Garnish: dehydrated lime wheel

Combine the rums, pandan syrup,
lime juice, and yuzu juice in a cocktail
shaker with ice. Shake and strain into
a coupe. Garnish with a dehydrated
lime wheel.

YUZU-SHIO DAIQUIRI

SERVES

ONE

COCKTAILS

91

CALPICO SWIZZLE

This exuberant swizzle gets its name from Calpico, a Japanese soft drink I loved during my childhood, which has a milky, yogurt-like flavor. It gets a decidedly more adult kick with the addition of fragrant gin and *nigori* sake, which is unfiltered and has a cloudy or milky appearance and a silky mouthfeel on the palate. A bit of blue curaçao keeps things vibrant, along with some bubbles from a dry sparkling wine, and this colorful drink is garnished with a bright red cocktail cherry. At Katana Kitten, we prefer the cherries from the brand Filthy Food, since their vibrant color is natural. A sprinkling of freshly ground sansho peppercorns imparts a unique aroma.

¾ ounce Bombay Sapphire East gin

¾ ounce nigori sake

¾ ounce Calpico concentrate (available at Japanese markets or online)

¼ ounce Giffard blue curaçao liqueur

¼ ounce simple syrup (see page 56)

½ ounce fresh lime juice

¾ ounce blanc de blanc sparkling wine (a dry bubbly may be substituted)

Garnish: cocktail cherry, freshly ground sansho peppercorns, fresh mint sprigs

SERVES

ONE

Combine the gin, sake, Calpico, curaçao, simple syrup, lime juice, and sparkling wine in a pearl diver–style or collins glass. Fill the glass three-quarters full with pebble ice or crushed ice. Using a swizzle stick or a barspoon, stir to combine. Mound more pebble ice or crushed ice on top of the drink. Garnish with a cocktail cherry, freshly ground sansho peppercorns, and mint sprigs.

PANDAN SYRUP

Makes 2 cups

1¼ cups water
1¼ cups sugar
2 whole pandan leaves

In a small saucepan, combine the water and sugar and heat over medium heat, stirring to dissolve the sugar. Add the pandan leaves and bring the mixture to a simmer. Remove from the heat, cover, and let cool. Strain through cheesecloth into an airtight 1-pint glass container. Seal the container and store in the refrigerator for up to 6 weeks.

This is by far Katana Kitten's most copiously consumed drink. I named it after the adorable sweet bears found in Asia, and it is also a play on the word "pandan," an aromatic leaf that is a key ingredient that brings an earthy and nutty note to the drink. But most of all, it is a celebration of Calpico, the Japanese soft drink. It is actually a perfect modifier, as it brings sweetness that is balanced by a yogurt-like tang. Calpico also works as an emulsifier, like egg whites or cream, that binds all the different flavors and ingredients together and, when topped with soda, creates a delightfully frothy head. Finally, the Calpico lends the cocktail its white appearance, which we counterbalance with black lava salt on the rim, to re-create the colors of a panda's fur.

Black lava salt, for rimming the glass

Lemon wedge, for rimming the glass

1¼ ounces Suntory Haku vodka

½ ounce pear eau-de-vie

1 ounce Calpico concentrate (available in Japanese markets and online)

½ ounce fresh lemon juice

½ ounce Pandan Syrup (recipe at left)

Soda water, chilled

Rim a collins glass with black lava salt (see page 55). Combine the vodka, eau-de-vie, Calpico, lemon juice, and pandan syrup in a cocktail shaker with ice. Shake and strain into the prepared glass over ice cubes. Top with chilled soda water and stir gently.

PANDA
FIZZ

SERVES

ONE

COCKTAILS

COOL RUNNINGS

SERVES

ONE

The inspiration for this drink is the classic Mai Tai, a cocktail that conjures up beach vacations in many an imagination. I collaborated with one of our star bartenders, Laura McGinley, to give the drink a winter makeover. We named it Cool Runnings to salute the popular 1993 sports comedy of the same name about the improbable debut of the Jamaican bobsled team at the Alberta Winter Olympics. Batavia arrack provides some rummy funkiness and sweet potato shochu adds comforting notes of the baked, starchy tuber that go well with banana and chocolate. The Puffed Rice–Coconut Orgeat is the secret ingredient and adds a luxurious mouthfeel. For the garnish, we take Okinawan purple yams, slice them thinly, dehydrate the slices, then pulverize them into a powder that is replete with potato flavor and a stunning purple color.

¾ ounce Batavia arrack

¾ ounce Asahi-Mannen sweet potato shochu

¼ ounce Giffard crème de cacao

¼ ounce Giffard crème de banane

¾ ounce Puffed Rice–Coconut Orgeat (recipe follows)

½ ounce fresh lemon juice

Garnish: purple yam powder and toasted shaved coconut flakes.

Combine the arrack, shochu, crème de cacao, crème de banane, orgeat, and lemon juice in a cocktail shaker with ice. Shake until chilled and strain over pebble ice in a rocks glass. Mound more pebble ice on top of the drink. Garnish with yam powder and toasted shaved coconut flakes.

PUFFED RICE–COCONUT ORGEAT

Makes 2 cups

1¼ cups sugar

1¼ cups unsweetened coconut milk

¼ cup toasted cocoa nibs

½ cup roasted puffed genmai (brown rice)

¼ teaspoon orange flower water

¼ teaspoon almond extract

In a medium saucepan, combine the sugar, coconut milk, and cocoa nibs and heat over medium heat, stirring to dissolve the sugar. Add the puffed genmai and simmer for about 5 minutes, then remove from the heat and let cool. Strain through cheesecloth into an airtight 1-pint container glass and stir in the orange flower water and almond extract. Seal the container and store in the refrigerator for up to 2 weeks.

PURPLE YAM
POWDER
Makes 2 to 3 tablespoons

1 purple Okinawan yam
(about 1 pound)

Rinse and peel the yam,
then slice it thinly. Place
the slices in a dehydrator
and dehydrate them
completely. Blend the
slices into a powder
using a Vitamix or a spice
grinder. Transfer the
powder to an airtight
1-cup glass container.
Seal the container and
store in the freezer for up
to 1 year

OCTOBER

FIZZ

The origins of Oktoberfest date back to October 12, 1810, when Bavaria's future king Ludwig married Princess Theresa and graciously invited the people of Munich to celebrate in the fields by the city gate. Over the centuries, it has evolved into a massive annual festival, where millions of liters of beer are enthusiastically imbibed over a sixteen-day period. Beer and whisky are, of course, a delicious combination, playing off their shared DNA of malted barley. This cocktail, a take on a Chicago Fizz, is my way to salute the season. It is a concoction of whisky, port, Rock & Rye, squash puree, and, of course, a bit of beer. While I created it for fall, it is easy-drinking all year long.

1 ounce Mars Iwai 45 Japanese whisky

¾ ounce tawny port

½ ounce fresh lemon juice

½ ounce Mister Katz's Rock & Rye

¼ ounce simple syrup (see page 56)

¾ ounce egg white

SERVES

ONE

roasted pumpkin seeds

Combine the whisky, port, lemon juice, Rock & Rye, simple syrup, egg white, squash puree, and bitters in a cocktail shaker and dry shake without ice. Add ice and shake until chilled, then add the beer and gently swirl the shaker to incorporate it. Strain into a fizz glass containing an ice spear or a stack of ice cubes. Garnish with grated cinnamon and roasted pumpkin seeds.

RUBYFRUIT

This cocktail is named after a popular bar that used to occupy the space that is now Katana Kitten and is our way of showing of respect to those who came before us. The bar might be gone, but we do our best to honor its spirit and the people who kept it alive. The cocktail's inspiration is the frozen margarita, but what sets it apart is our housemade Tutti-Fruity Cordial. We combine all our bar fruit and veggie odds and ends to make a fruity cordial. It is part of the ethos in Japan that maximizes every ingredient, just as my grandma would carefully wrap even the smallest end piece of a fruit or vegetable and place it respectfully in her fridge. It is very satisfying to give these precious ingredients a full life.

Shichimi Salt (recipe follows), for rimming the glass

Lime wedge, for rimming the glass

1½ ounces Olmeca Altos Plata tequila

1 ounce Tutti-Fruity Cordial (recipe follows)

¾ ounce fresh lime juice

½ ounce ruby port wine

1 cup crushed ice

Garnish: seasonal fruit

Rim half a double old-fashioned glass with shichimi salt (see page 55). Combine the tequila, cordial, lime juice and crushed ice in a heavy-duty blender and blend until the mixture has a silky, slushy consistency. Pour into the prepared glass and float the ruby port on top. Garnish with seasonal fruit.

SERVES

ONE

TUTTI-FRUITY CORDIAL

Save bar fruit, vegetable, and herb odds and ends, such as the end cuts of citrus (including limes, lemons, and oranges), cucumber peels, trimmed herbs and vegetables, stone fruit pits, and bruised fruit that isn't appealing for garnishes, in a resealable plastic storage bag in the freezer to make this cordial. Makes 2 cups

1½ cups sugar
1 cup leftover bar fruit
1¼ cups water
½ teaspoon citric acid

Combine the sugar and leftover bar fruit in an airtight 1-quart glass container and refrigerate for 24 hours. Add the water to the mix, stir to dissolve the sugar, and add the citric acid. Strain through cheesecloth into a clean 1-quart glass container. Seal the container and store in the refrigerator for up to 1 month.

SHICHIMI SALT

Makes 1 cup

½ cup shichimi togarashi
½ cup Maldon salt
Zest of 1 lemon, grated
using a Microplane

Combine the shichimi
togarashi, salt, and lemon
zest in a mortar and use
the pestle to combine
the mixture. Transfer
to an airtight 1-cup
glass container. Seal
the container and
store in the pantry for
up to 1 year.

BOILERMAKERS

HAVING BOILERMAKERS, THE CLASSIC PAIRING OF A BEER with a shot, on our menu is our way of honoring James Tune of Boilermaker, whose vision of a Japanese-American bar was brought to life as Katana Kitten. The pairing, if you believe cocktail lore, traces back to the days of steam locomotive workers who would enjoy one after a grueling factory shift. For something so momentous, we wanted drinks that were a bit more unique and interesting than a simple beer and a shot, although we love that classic combination as well. While whiskey is traditionally the shot of choice, at Katana Kitten, we again take creative and playful liberties.

FANCY RAMUNE

Ramune is an iconic lemon-lime soda in Japan that for me brings up very nostalgic feelings about summer festivals of long ago and coming home. To this day, it comes in a cool bottle with a glass marble stuck in the top of the neck that you have to push down in order to sip the soda. The flavor profile of Ramune was our inspiration here, only we make a very fancy version from scratch. It is a bit of a lemon-drop-meets-sake-bomb, pairing Other Half Forever Ever IPA, which is an unfiltered, zesty and dry style of American IPA, with a chilled shot of our house Lemon-Daiginjo made with Dassai 50 *junmai daiginjo* sake and lemon sherbet for a refreshing take on a shandy.

16 ounces Other Half Forever Ever IPA (or another local citrusy IPA)

1 shot chilled Lemon-Daiginjo (recipe follows)

Serve the IPA in a pint glass accompanied by a chilled shot of Lemon-Daiginjo.

LEMON-DAIGINJO

Makes 2½ cups

1 cup Dassai 50 junmai daiginjo sake

¾ cup Housemade Lemon Sherbet (recipe follows)

¾ cup Lemon Stock (recipe follows)

Combine the sake, sherbet, and lemon stock in an airtight 1-quart glass container. Seal the container and store in the refrigerator for up to 1 week.

HOUSEMADE LEMON SHERBET

Makes 2 cups

Zest of 8 lemons, cut into strips with a peeler or paring knife

1½ cups sugar

1½ cups fresh lemon juice (see note)

NOTE: *Reserve the spent peels to make the Lemon Stock (recipe follows).*

In a medium bowl, muddle the lemon zest with the sugar, cover, and let stand for 1 hour. Add the lemon juice and stir to dissolve the sugar. Strain through cheesecloth into an airtight 1-pint glass container. Seal the container and store in the refrigerator for up to 2 weeks.

SERVES

ONE

LEMON STOCK

RECIPE ADAPTED FROM TRASH TIKI'S IAIN GRIFFITHS

Makes 2 cups

4 cups water

3 cups lemon peels (reserved from making Lemon Sherbet)

1½ teaspoons sugar

1/8 teaspoon citric acid

In a large stockpot, combine the water and lemon husks and bring to a gentle simmer over medium heat. Simmer for 5 minutes. Using a chinois, strain the liquid into another pot, squeezing the husks to maximize their output, and cook over medium heat until the liquid has reduced by half. Strain through cheesecloth into an airtight 1-pint glass container, then stir in the sugar and citric acid until dissolved. Seal the container and store in the refrigerator for up to 2 weeks.

HAIR OF THE CAT

SERVES

O N E

The name is a play on "hair of the dog" (or dragon or tiger, as I'm sure you have heard many variations out there, if you are prone to overindulging), that spirited tradition of having a morning-after pick-me-up of whatever you were drinking the night before that got you into your current predicament. We pair Sixpoint Brewery Alpenflo lager with Cat Bran, our own take on the famed Denki Bran from Tokyo's historic Kamiya Bar. To make Cat Bran, we infuse American brandy with spices, including juniper berries, cinnamon, and black cardamom. Denki Bran is around 25% ABV and the brandy is 50%, so we bring down the latter's proof with a mix of teas—chamomile, Assam, strawberry, and mint—and add a bit of sugar. The tea and spices all work well together, and the lager has a tea undertone. But best of all, when I serve it, I get to tell the Denki Bran story and explain Kamiya Bar's important role in Japanese cocktail history.

16 ounces Sixpoint Brewery Alpenflo lager

1 shot chilled Cat Bran (recipe follows)

Serve the lager in a pint glass accompanied by a chilled shot of Cat Bran.

CAT BRAN

Makes 2 cups

1 cup Spice-Infused Brandy (recipe follows)

1 cup Fruit Tea Mixture (recipe follows)

¼ cup sugar

Combine the brandy, tea mixture, and sugar in an airtight 1-pint glass container. Stir to dissolve the sugar. Seal the container and store in the refrigerator for up to 1 month.

SPICE-INFUSED BRANDY

Makes 750ml

1 (750ml) bottle The Christian Bros. Sacred Bond brandy

1½ teaspoons fresh juniper berries, cracked

1 cinnamon stick

1 black cardamom pod

Combine the brandy, juniper berries, cinnamon stick, and cardamom pod in an airtight 1-quart glass container and steep, covered, at room temperature for 48 hours. Strain into the brandy original bottle and store in the pantry for up to 1 year.

FRUIT TEA MIXTURE

Makes 2 cups

1 tablespoon loose
chamomile tea

1 tablespoon loose
strawberry tea

1 tablespoon loose mint
tea

1½ teaspoons loose black
tea leaves

2¼ cups room-
temperature water

Combine the teas and
water in an airtight 1-pint
glass container and steep
at room temperature
for 1 to 2 hours. Strain
through cheesecloth
into a clean 1-pint glass
container. Seal the
container and store in
the refrigerator for up
to 1 week.

ICHI-MAS

Ichi-Mas is, by far, our number one bestselling boilermaker. The name is a made-up phrase coined by Naren Young, my American bartending sensei. *Ichi* means "one" in Japanese and *mas* is "more" in Spanish, so essentially it means "one more." We pair a frigid shot of Suntory Toki whisky from the highball machine with a watermelon slice seasoned with shichimi salt. This harkens back to my days at The Daily, which had a drink on the menu called the Soup du Jour. It consisted of a whiskey that changed on a daily basis and was served neat in a rocks glass with an orange or watermelon slice on the side. Our fruit-topped shot is accompanied by an icy can of Sapporo beer. Guests take the shot of whisky and a bite of the cold watermelon, followed by a guzzle of cold beer.

1 shot cold Suntory Toki whisky

Shichimi salt (page 101)

Watermelon slice

1 can Sapporo beer, chilled

Serve the shot of cold Suntory Toki topped by a shichimi-salt sprinkled watermelon slice and accompanied by a can of cold Sapporo beer.

SERVES

ONE

BOILERMAKERS

LERMAYER

SERVES

FOUR

This boilermaker is very close to my heart and is my homage to the late John Lermayer, a charismatic bartending legend who put Miami firmly on the craft cocktail map while bringing each one of us in this industry closer together. It was the first drink that I conceptualized for Katana Kitten's menu, and we were going to spring it on John when he came to see our bar opening, as he always liked surprises. We got the news of his sudden passing at age forty-five while we were training Katana Kitten's bar team at Boilermaker, our sister bar. There are so many times that we find ourselves doing fun things and making memorable nights at Katana Kitten and wishing that John could have experienced them in person. The pairing is John's classic Bubble Back, a shot of tequila chased by Champagne, Krug specifically. Greg Boehm, on behalf of Katana Kitten, set up a college fund for John's son, Radek, and all proceeds from sales of this drink go to the fund. John's legacy will live on for a long time in our small bar in the West Village.

½ bottle Krug Grande Cuvée Champagne

4 shots Olmeca Altos Plata tequila

Seasonal fruit

Fill a large cypress bowl with crushed ice. On top of the ice, arrange the ½ bottle of Krug, the four shots of tequila, and the seasonal fruits as garnishes.

MAXIMILIAN

This pairing is for my friend Max Warner, who represented Chivas Regal for more than a decade as its global brand ambassador. I was absolutely privileged to get to know him after I won the Chivas Masters global cocktail competition in 2014. I'm grateful for memories of spending a great deal of time with him in Tokyo and many different parts of the world. He has long inspired me, both as a bartender and as someone who knows how to entertain guests with ease. The spirit we use here is Chivas Regal 18, which happens to be a favorite of many bartenders. Given that it is a very rich whisky with notes of apple and dried fruit, it goes really well with cider. We pair the shot with seasonal ciders from Downeast Cider House. During the summer, we serve their Aloha Fridays, a pineapple cider. In winter, we switch to their Winter Spice cider. Our guests at Katana Kitten love this pairing year round.

1 shot Chivas Regal 18

12 ounces Downeast Cider House cider, chilled

Serve the shot of Chivas Regal accompanied by a glass of the cider.

SERVES

ONE

BOILERMAKERS

WITH A LITTLE

HELP

FROM MY FRIENDS

While I'm best known for my work at Katana Kitten, throughout my bartending career, I have created scores of recipes for other bars and events that were influenced by Japanese bartending and ingredients from Japan, the best of which I share in the pages that follow. They are joined by recipes from bartending stars in Japan, as well as those in the US, who honor this approach as well.

4

SOME OF MY

FAVORITE

CREATIONS

THE FOLLOWING ARE SOME OF MY FAVORITE RECIPES, developed over my years of working as a bartender in New York City. As you will see, they all take inspiration from Japan and its drinking traditions.

AGUA VERDE

This phrase means "green water" in Spanish, and the inspiration of this cocktail is *agua fresca*, a traditional Mexican soft drink. Living in New York City introduced me to Mexican culture and its rich culinary traditions. Visiting Mexico rocket-charged my love and respect for their flavors, as did the discovery of the large colorful glass jars containing a variety of freshly made *aguas frescas*. For a Japanese spin, I added shishito peppers, which are served grilled in just about every yakitori restaurant and izakaya in Japan. They have become ubiquitous in New York City restaurants in recent years as well. These small peppers are concentrated with a bright green flavor and bring a vibrant color that lends the cocktail its name. I moved to New York City in 2008 and noticed a certain trend among restaurants, with particular vegetables gaining huge popularity and seeming to pop up on every menu across town. This happened with cauliflower, Brussels sprouts, and, of course, kale. We recently experienced a shishito pepper bonanza, and I was quite happy about it.

Matcha Salt (recipe follows), for rimming the glass

Lime wedge, for rimming the glass

1 ounce Montelobos mezcal joven

½ ounce iichiko Saiten shochu

1 barspoon Italicus Rosolio di Bergamotto bergamot liqueur

5 ounces Kabosu Lemonade (recipe follows)

¼ ounce fresh shishito pepper juice

Pinch of sea salt

Garnish: chargrilled shishito pepper

Rim half of a pilsner glass with matcha salt (see page 55). Build the cocktail in the prepared glass by adding the mezcal, shochu, bergamot liqueur, and lemonade over ice. Stir until chilled. Float the shishito pepper juice and salt over the top of the cocktail. Garnish with a chargrilled shishito pepper.

RECIPE CONTINUES

SERVES ONE

MATCHA SALT

Makes ½ cup

½ cup Maldon salt

1 teaspoon matcha green tea powder

Combine the salt and matcha in an airtight glass 1-cup container. Seal the container and store in the pantry for up to 1 year.

KABOSU LEMONADE

Makes 2 cups

¼ cup Lime Oleo-Saccharum (recipe follows)

1 ounce kabosu juice

3 ounces fresh lemon juice

1½ cups water

Put the lime oleo-saccharum in an airtight 1-pint glass container, add the kabosu and lemon juices, and stir to dissolve. Add the water and stir well. This is best when made to order but can be made in advance and stored in the refrigerator for up to 1 day.

LIME OLEO-SACCHARUM

Makes 1 cup

Zest of 5 limes, cut into strips with a peeler or paring knife

1 cup sugar

In a large bowl, muddle the lime zest with sugar, then transfer to an airtight 1-cup glass container. Seal the container and store in the pantry for up to 2 months.

AKA
RANGER

SERVES

ONE

124

This cocktail takes its cues from hot toddies and mulled wine and is based on shochu, Japan's national spirit. While *oyuwari,* namely mixing with hot water, is a popular way to enjoy shochu back home, I use a mulled wine to add a festive note to the drink. *Aka* means "red" in Japanese and reminds me of the autumn leaves in my hometown. Drinking this while watching the animated Japanese TV series *Five Rangers* that we all enjoyed growing up brings back a lot of countryside memories.

1 ounce Yamasemi rice shochu

¼ ounce crème de cassis

¼ ounce Rich Honey Syrup (recipe follows)

1 dash Sangostura Bitters (recipe follows)

Hot Jasmine Mulled Wine (recipe follows)

Garnish: star anise pod

In a Japanese teacup, combine the shochu, crème de cassis, honey syrup, and bitters. Top with hot mulled wine. Garnish with a star anise pod.

RICH HONEY SYRUP

Makes 1 cup

⅔ cup honey

⅓ cup water

In a small saucepan, combine the honey and water and heat over medium-low heat, stirring until the honey has fully dissolved. Let cool, then pour into an airtight 1-cup glass container. Seal the container and store in the refrigerator for up to 2 months.

SANGOSTURA BITTERS

Makes 16 ounces

1 (16-ounce) bottle Angostura bitters

¼ cup sansho peppercorns

Combine the bitters and peppercorns in an airtight 1-pint glass container and steep, covered, for 48 hours. Strain into the original bitters bottle and store in the pantry for up to 6 months.

HOT JASMINE MULLED WINE

Makes 1 quart

1 (750ml) bottle semi-dry Riesling wine

3 Bosc pears, sliced

1 cinnamon stick

Zest of 1 lemon, cut into strips with a peeler or paring knife

1 tablespoon sugar

1 cup white port wine

1 tablespoon loose jasmine pearl tea leaves

In a saucepan, combine the wine, pears, cinnamon stick, lemon zest, and sugar and bring to a gentle simmer over medium-low heat. Cook for 15 minutes, then let cool. Strain through cheesecloth into a 1-quart glass container and add the white port and jasmine tea leaves. Steep for 3 minutes, then strain into an airtight 1-quart glass container. Seal the container and store in the refrigerator for up to 1 month.

ANBAI

Fill an old-fashioned glass with ice. Build the drink by adding the Empirical Spirits Onyx Blend, tea, sake, and mezcal. Express a lemon twist over the drink and discard, then garnish with shio kombu.

RED SHISO TEA

Makes 2 cups

2 cups water
15 fresh red shiso leaves
¾ cup sugar
½ teaspoon citric acid

Bring the water to a boil in a small pot, heat the water until boiling. Add the shiso leaves, remove from the heat, and steep for 5 minutes. Strain through cheesecloth into an airtight 1-pint glass container. Add the sugar and stir to dissolve, then add the citric acid, which will turn the tea bright red. Seal the container and store in the refrigerator for up to 1 week.

London bar phenom team Ryan Chetiyawardana and Iain Griffiths are known for venues that balance creativity and sustainability. The two, together with their global bar director Alex Lawrence, briefly graced New York City with an elaborate across-the-pond pop-up of Lyaness, the bold concept that succeeded the globally acclaimed Dandelyan. I was delighted that Iain Griffiths invited me to do a guest shift and created this cocktail for the occasion. I called it Anbai, which is grandma talk for creating the perfect balance of taste, whether by adding a pinch of salt or a smidgen of sugar. The base of the cocktail is Empirical Spirits Onyx; developed in collaboration with Lyaness, this unique koji-based spirit also incorporates hibiscus and birchwood kombucha. To provide its vibrant scarlet color, I use red shiso, which is a traditional culinary colorant in Japan. With a bit of citrus acidity, it literally turns bright purple-red. This particular umeshu is based on sake and is *muto*, meaning it contains no added sugar, which delivers the aromatic acidity of the plum. A touch of special mezcal adds a hint of earthiness that puts this cocktail over the top.

1 ounce Empirical Spirits Onyx Blend

1 ounce Red Shiso Tea (recipe at left)

1 ounce Nanbu Bijin Muto umeshu plum sake

1 barspoon Del Maguey Tobalá mezcal

Garnish: lemon twist and *shio kombu* (seasoned Japanese kelp)

SERVES

ONE

SOME OF MY FAVORITE CREATIONS

127

AZUSA
EXPRESS

Azusa is the name of our precious daughter, my little pride and joy. While Azusa is also the inspiration behind this cocktail, it's actually a popular traditional name in Japan, in addition to being the name of a Japanese cherry birch tree with beautiful white flowers that blossom each spring. In Nagano, there are many azusa trees, and the train that passes through there from Tokyo is named the Azusa Express, which is quite poetic. The drink itself is my version of the cosmopolitan, the cocktail that was first perfected and popularized by Toby Cecchini during his tenure at Odeon in the late 1980s. In this version, instead of using cranberry juice, the color and tartness of fresh cranberries are added to aquavit via sous vide.

1½ ounces Cranberry Sous-Vide Aquavit (recipe follows)

½ ounce Reisetbauer apple eau-de-vie

¾ ounce Combier liqueur

¾ ounce fresh lemon juice

½ ounce simple syrup (see page 56)

¼ barspoon umeboshi (pickled plum) puree

Garnish: edible flower

Combine the aquavit, eau-de-vie, Combier, lemon juice, simple syrup, and umeboshi puree in a cocktail shaker with ice. Shake until chilled and fine-strain into a chilled coupe. Garnish with an edible flower.

SERVES

ONE

CRANBERRY SOUS-VIDE AQUAVIT
Makes 750mL

1 (750ml) bottle Svöl aquavit
1½ cups fresh cranberries
1 teaspoon sugar
Pinch of salt

Combine the aquavit, cranberries, sugar, and salt in an ROP bag and vacuum seal to remove all the air. Cook in a water bath using an immersion circulator at 135°F for 1½ hours. Remove and let cool. Strain through cheesecloth into the original aquavit bottle and store in the refrigerator for up to 2 months.

CROWN HEIGHTS

This drink, my version of a Manhattan, came about by kicking around ideas with my partner in crime, Nacho. What makes it stand out is its clear color, which is completely unexpected for a cocktail that usually has a deep mahogany tone. I did this by subbing out the usual bourbon or rye whiskey for unaged whiskey and genever. It is still a rich and luxurious sip. Suze, a gentian-forward French herbal liqueur, balances the sweetness with earthy bitterness and adds a beautiful yellow hue. It's named after the Brooklyn neighborhood where my wife, Taryn, and I first lived together.

1 ounce George Dickel No. 1 white corn whisky

1 ounce Old Duff genever single malt

1 ounce Dolin Blanc vermouth

½ ounce Suze gentiane liqueur

1 barspoon Luxardo maraschino liqueur

3 dashes yuzu bitters

Garnish: orange twist

Combine the whisky, genever, vermouth, Suze, maraschino liqueur, and bitters in a mixing glass with ice. Stir until chilled and strain into a chilled small coupe. Garnish with an orange twist.

SERVES

ONE

131

DREAM-CATCHER

SERVES

ONE

This is a summertime highball variation that I created for High West Distillery, a whiskey producer in Park City, Utah, that I admire for its wonderful blended whiskeys, especially their peaty Campfire expression. Sometimes with whiskey, I notice there are tropical notes, and I chose to highlight this quality by creating a cocktail with passion fruit and yuzu. I added vermouth to lighten its body, and the coconut rim further amplifies these tropical notes, imparted by aging in American oak barrels.

Coconut Salt (recipe follows), for rimming the glass

Lemon wedge, for rimming the glass

1 ounce High West Campfire whiskey

1 ounce Dolin Blanc vermouth

¾ ounce Passion Fruit-Yuzu Sour Mix (recipe follows)

Fever-Tree Sparkling Lemon

Garnish: Coconut Salt and dehydrated lemon slice

Rim a highball glass with coconut salt (see page 55). Combine the whiskey, vermouth, and sour mix in a cocktail shaker with ice. Shake and strain into a highball glass over an ice spear or stack of ice cubes. Top with sparkling lemonade and gently stir. Garnish with coconut salt and dehydrated lemon slice.

PASSION FRUIT-YUZU SOUR MIX
Makes 2½ cups

1 cup passion fruit puree

½ cup yuzu juice

1 cup simple syrup (see page 56)

Combine the passion fruit puree, yuzu juice, and simple syrup in an airtight 1-quart glass container. Seal the container and store in the refrigerator for up to 1 month.

COCONUT SALT
Makes 1½ cups

1 cup unsweetened shredded coconut

½ cup Maldon salt

Combine the coconut flakes and salt in a mortar and grind together with a pestle. Pour into an airtight 1-quart glass container. Seal the container and store in the pantry for up to 1 year.

SOME OF MY FAVORITE CREATIONS

LAPSANG SOUCHONG TEA-INFUSED LILLET ROUGE

Makes 750ml

1 (750ml) bottle Lillet Rouge

3 tablespoons loose Lapsang Souchong tea leaves

Combine the Lillet Rouge and tea leaves in an airtight 1-quart glass container and steep at room temperature for 45 minutes. Strain through cheesecloth into the original Lillet bottle and store in the refrigerator for up to 2 months.

I named this cocktail after the famous mountains that lie between Nagano and Yamanashi Prefectures. They are called the Yatsugatake, meaning "eight peaks," referring to the major mountains in the range that climbers try to summit. In this lower-ABV aperitif, I split the base between umeshu and Lillet Rouge infused with Lapsang Souchong tea. The tea's origin is a mountainous region of China, where it is dried, fermented, and smoked over pinewood fires in baskets, and it imbues the cocktail with a rich, piney, and smoky note.

1 ounce Choya umeshu

1 ounce Lapsang Souchong Tea-Infused Lillet Rouge (recipe at left)

Soda water, chilled

Garnish: blood orange slice

Build the drink in a collins glass, adding the umeshu and tea-infused Lillet Rouge over an ice spear or a stack of ice cubes. Top with chilled soda water and gently stir. Garnish with a blood orange slice.

EIGHT PEAKS

SERVES

ONE

135

FRIDAY IN
THE PARK

This vermouth highball variation has its origins in the time I spent working behind the bar together with Nacho at The Daily. We would peruse old cocktail books and experiment with recipes, and one of our favorite creations was housemade vermouth, which is essentially aromatized wine. We found out that it is really not difficult to make from scratch. We wanted something hyper-local, so we used a dry Riesling from New York's Finger Lakes region. From our community garden in Brooklyn Heights, I harvested wormwood, lavender, and rose petals, to which I added coriander seeds, citrus zests, and other botanicals. These were combined with the wine and allowed to macerate for about a week. Once the botanicals were strained out, we added sugar and a bit of apple eau-de-vie from upstate New York to fortify and preserve it. I recommend storing it refrigerated all the time, as you would with any wine.

2 ounces Homemade Vermouth (recipe follows)

4 ounces Doc's Draft hard pear cider

Garnish: fresh herbs and lemon twist

Pour the vermouth and cider into a wineglass filled with ice and stir to combine. Garnish with fresh herbs. Express a lemon twist over the drink and discard.

HOMEMADE VERMOUTH

Makes 750ml

1 (750ml) bottle dry Riesling wine

¾ cup wormwood

1 stalk fresh lemongrass

2 tablespoons finely chopped fresh angelica root

10 fresh green shiso leaves

Zest of ½ grapefruit, cut into strips with a peeler or paring knife

Zest of 2 lemons, cut into strips with a peeler or paring knife

2 teaspoons dried culinary-grade rose petals

1½ teaspoons dried lavender

5 fresh lavender sprigs

1½ tablespoons dried licorice root

4 fresh sage leaves

1 teaspoon sansho peppercorns

Pinch of sea salt

¾ ounce grape or other fruit eau-de-vie

1½ tablespoons sugar

1 tablespoon raw honey

Combine the Riesling, wormwood, lemongrass, angelica root, shiso leaves, grapefruit and lemon zests, rose petals, lavender, licorice, sage leaves, peppercorns, and salt in an airtight 1-quart glass container. Cover and let stand at room temperature for 1 week. Strain through cheesecloth into a clean 1-quart glass container. Add the eau-de-vie, sugar, and honey. Cover and let stand at room temperature for several days. Transfer to the original Riesling bottle and store in the refrigerator for up to 1 year.

SERVES

ONE

GOMA COLADA

Everyone loves a piña colada. I'm particularly fond of its silky texture, creaminess, and tropical flavors. To give this cocktail a Japanese makeover, my inspiration was the use of *goma* (sesame seeds). In this cocktail, I use sesame paste, which adds a rich and complex sesame flavor.

½ ounce Black Sesame–Kokutou Cane Puree (recipe follows), plus more for painting the glass

¾ ounce Banks 5 Island rum

¾ ounce Cor Cor Green Okinawan rum or Rhum Clément Première Canne

½ ounce cream sherry

1½ ounces Pineapple Puree (recipe follows)

1½ ounces Coco López and Amazake Mix (recipe follows)

½ ounce fresh lime juice

Garnish: pineapple leaf and red cherry

Prepare a hurricane glass by painting Black Sesame and Kokutou. Paint stripes on its interior. Fill with pebble ice.

Combine the Banks 5 Island rum, Okinawan rum, sherry, pineapple puree, Coco López and Amazake Mix, lime juice, and cane puree in a cocktail shaker and shake until chilled. Pour into the prepared hurricane glass. Garnish with a pineapple leaf and a red cherry.

PINEAPPLE PUREE
Makes 2 cups

1 cup pineapple juice

1 cup fresh pineapple chunks

Combine the ingredients in a heavy-duty blender and puree. Pour into an airtight container. Store in the refrigerator for up to 3 days.

COCO LÓPEZ AND AMAZAKE MIX
Makes 2 cups

1¼ cups Coco López cream of coconut

5 ounces amazake (a kind of low-alcohol sake)

Combine the ingredients in an airtight 1-pint glass container. Store in the refrigerator up to 1 week.

BLACK SESAME AND KOKUTOU PUREE
Makes 1½ cups

1 cup kokutou (Japanese dark cane sugar)

½ cup water

3 tablespoons black sesame paste

In a small saucepan, combine the kokutou and water and heat over medium heat, stirring to dissolve. Add the sesame paste and stir to incorporate. Let cool, then pour into an airtight container. Store in the refrigerator for up to 1 month.

SERVES ONE

INAGO

SOME OF MY FAVORITE CREATIONS

SERVES

ONE

With its name meaning "grasshopper" in Japanese, this variation on the classic dessert cocktail of the same name is amped up by a full-bodied American bourbon, along with a hint of smoke from an Islay single malt whisky. While still taking the balance and identity of this drink from the Grasshopper, this cocktail is built based on my sense memory of the rice harvest season in Minowa. Kinako sugar brings a sweet, malty aroma that reminds me of milling rice husks, and the peatiness of the Scotch conjures the burning of dry hay in the fields.

Bowmore 18-year-old single malt Scotch whisky

Kinako Sugar (recipe follows)

½ ounce Elijah Craig Small Batch bourbon

1 ounce Giffard crème de châtaigne

1 ounce Giffard crème de cacao

1½ ounces half-and-half

Using an atomizer, spray the inside and one side of the outside of a chilled coupe or Nick & Nora glass with the whisky and dust the sprayed side with the sugar. Combine the bourbon, crème de châtaigne, crème de cacao, and half-and-half in a cocktail shaker with ice. Shake until chilled and strain into the prepared glass.

KINAKO SUGAR
Makes 2 cups

1 cup kinako (toasted soybean flour)
1 cup confectioners' sugar

Combine the kinako and sugar in an airtight 1-pint glass container. Seal the container and store in the pantry for up to 1 year.

ON RICE PADDIES AND GRASSHOPPERS

My family has several rice paddies back in Minowa, so I grew up eating our local harvest from birth until I moved to Tokyo. Even then, my family sent me care packages of our family rice. Each year, the grain has two major events: planting in the spring and harvesting in the fall. The paddies are first flooded, then rice seedlings are planted. During the summer, there are heavy showers and scorching sun, and the rice grows abundantly. In the fall, you begin to see the rice grains on the stalks. At harvest time, the paddies are dried out completely and the harvesting work is done with a combine. But back in the day, it was harvested by hand with a *kama,* a curved machete, which was back-breaking work.

Once the rice was harvested, a second harvest would begin: the hundreds of grasshoppers that had populated the paddy. You catch them by the handful and put them in a sack that you wrap around your waist. My grandma would then cook them in sweet soy sauce, sugar, salt, and mirin. They were absolutely delicious. This is something you'd rarely see in cities—just in the countryside, where they are a local delicacy. I once brought a batch back to New York City and shared it with my good friend Nacho, who grew up eating *chapulines* in Mexico. He loved the dish, and together we discovered how well it accompanied a Highland reposado tequila.

JAPANESE HIGHBALL

SERVES

ONE

When you order a highball in Japan, it is universally implied that you are ordering a whisky highball. The drink is very personal, and this is how I prefer making them at home. In Japan, after a long day's work, people head to their local bar or izakaya and order beer and whisky highballs. This is a great pairing with the izakaya's fried and salty snacks, which beg for a refreshing accompaniment. Moreover, at around $5 a pop, it is completely democratic and popular across all demographics. My version is the Platonic ideal of simplicity and deliciousness. The trick is to keep your Japanese whisky in the freezer and your seltzer in the fridge. While at the bar we obsess about ice, ordinary store-bought bagged ice will do just fine here. If your whisky is room temperature, stir it over the ice to bring it down in temperature. If it is coming from the freezer, as I prefer, stir it to raise the temperature and make the spirit amenable to proper dilution. Then add whatever fizzy water you have on hand, provided it is straight from the fridge. The drink takes literally seconds to throw together and enjoy. It is great as an aperitif, a meal accompaniment, or just for kicking back and watching the game or a movie. *Kanpai!*

Suntory Kakubin, strategically stored in the home freezer (feel free to substitute your favorite whisky)

Vintage seltzer or Q club soda (feel free to substitute your favorite fizzy water), well chilled

Garnish: lemon twist

Pour the kakubin into a tumbler filled with ice. Top with chilled soda water and gently stir. Express a lemon twist over the drink and discard.

KAHLÚA
MILK
PUNCH

MAKES

TWO

QUARTS

TWENTY

SERVINGS

This is a very complex and flavorful punch that I created originally for a StarChefs event in New York City. So if you find yourself entertaining a large group of friends or family, this is something you take your time to prepare in advance, but it is well worth the effort. My inspiration was my youth in Japan, when Kahlúa and milk was everyone's favorite drink. This version is a take on Mary Rockett's classic clarified milk punch, which has the sophistication, complexity, and finesse of each ingredient through maceration. The recipe was brought to my attention in Dave Wondrich's definitive book on the flowing bowl, *Punch*. This perfectly clear punch has a long mixological heritage and was a way to preserve milk by removing the proteins and fat solids that would otherwise spoil. The fact that it has a good alcoholic kick as a further preservative makes it irresistible to cocktail fans. The technique is finding renewed popularity today, as it creates a symphony of flavors that are perfectly melded together. I chose as my base a Highland Scotch whisky with classic Speyside rich malt sweetness and spice from sherry cask aging. Aged rum adds a roundness to the flavor and also brings baking spice aromas, like vanilla and cinnamon, from resting in American oak barrels. The milk emulsifies all the ingredients and smooths out any edges to the alcohol. To create the maximum intensity of coffee flavor, I use dark roasted espresso beans, as well as Kahlúa. Lastly, tamari adds a savory note that complements its sweetness, like sprinkling a bit of salt into hot chocolate.

¾ cup sugar

1¼ cups brewed coffee, hot

1½ cups Aberlour 12-year-old single malt Scotch whisky

1½ cups Bacardí Reserva Ocho rum

6 ounces Kahlúa coffee liqueur

5 ounces fresh lemon juice

½ ounce tamari

2 tablespoons cocoa nibs

2 tablespoons whole coffee beans

2 cups whole milk

Zest of 1 lemon, cut into strips with a peeler or paring knife

Garnish: 3 coffee beans and grated nutmeg for each serving

In a large bowl, stir together the sugar and the hot coffee to dissolve the sugar. Let cool, then stir in the whisky, rum, Kahlúa, lemon juice, and tamari. In a saucepan, toast the cocoa nibs and coffee beans over medium-low heat, continuously moving the pan, for about 3 minutes. Turn off the heat and let cool. Add the milk and lemon zest to the saucepan and slowly bring to a simmer over medium-low heat. Remove from the heat add the whisky mixture. Stir well, and allow to cool, then rest overnight in the fridge. Strain the mixture through cheesecloth into 2-quart container, squeezing the cheesecloth to extract all the liquid. Strain through a doubled coffee filter into a 2-quart bottle. The mixture should be perfectly clear, but there might be some sediment on the bottle. Store in the refrigerator for up to 2 weeks.

To serve, pour the punch into a brandy snifter over ice and stir. Garnish with 3 coffee beans and grated nutmeg.

KAKINOKI

The inspiration for this cocktail is a classic drink from New Orleans, the Sazerac, which is very spirit-forward. In keeping with its provenance, I wanted to use exclusively American spirits. To give it a Japanese flair, I call for a fresh yuzu twist. Yuzu is traditionally available in fall and winter, but it is now grown in California. At around $3 for a small fruit, its aromatic zest is incomparable. *Kakinoki* means "persimmon tree" in Japanese. Back home in Minowa, there is an abundance of these trees behind our family home and on the hillside of the nearby mountains. My grandma used to pick persimmons to prepare *hoshi gaki,* which consisted of the fruit being peeled, smoked, and dried in long rows outside, creating a picturesque orange curtain.

1¼ ounces Bertoux brandy

1¼ ounces Old Overholt rye whiskey

½ ounce Apologue Persimmon bittersweet liqueur

1 barspoon date syrup

3 dashes Sangostura Bitters (see page 125)

3 dashes Peychaud's bitters

Garnish: yuzu twist

Combine the brandy, whiskey, persimmon liqueur, date syrup, and both bitters in a mixing glass with ice. Stir until chilled and strain into a chilled rocks glass. Express a yuzu twist over the drink and discard.

SERVES

ONE

KURUMI

Fall is one of my favorite seasons, and I wanted to include a drink that embodies the overall sensation of autumn. My mind immediately raced to *kurumi*, which are Japanese walnuts that lend the cocktail its name. As the leaves turn with the season, the walnuts fall from the trees, and people happily gather them up. I have many fond memories of my grandma sitting beside a big pile of walnuts, carefully cracking them open and harvesting the lovely nut within, which she transformed into a beautiful sauce for *mochi* (rice cakes). The cocktail itself is my take on the classic Japanese cocktail that was included in Jerry Thomas's 1862 book *How to Mix Drinks, or The Bon-Vivant's Companion.* Ironically, there is nothing specifically Japanese about the Japanese cocktail, except its back story. Cocktail historian and friend of the bar David Wondrich theorizes that the drink was created to celebrate a visit by Japan's first diplomatic mission to the US following the opening of Japan. The delegation found friendly refuge in Thomas's bar and was led by Tateishi "Tommy" Onojirou Noriyuki, who earned quite a reputation as a bon vivant. In my version of this simple cocktail, I stay true to the classic with a Cognac base. Walnuts are incorporated into a lovely orgeat syrup and the cocktail's pleasing nuttiness is further amplified with pecan bitters.

2 ounces Rémy Martin 1738 Accord Royal Cognac

½ ounce Kurumi Orgeat (recipe follows)

3 dashes Miracle Mile toasted pecan bitters

Garnish: lemon twist

Combine the cognac, orgeat, and bitters in a mixing glass with ice. Stir and strain into a chilled Nick & Nora glass. Garnish with a lemon twist.

KURUMI ORGEAT
Makes 2 cups

1 cup blanched walnuts
1½ cups water
1¾ cups sugar
¾ ounce Cognac
¼ teaspoon orange flower water
¼ teaspoon almond extract

In a bowl, soak the walnuts in water to cover for 1 hour. Drain the walnuts and crush them in a Robot Coupe or food processor. In a small saucepan, combine the 1½ cups water, sugar, and crushed walnuts and bring to a simmer over medium heat, stirring to dissolve the sugar. Remove from the heat and let cool, then puree the mixture in a heavy-duty blender. Let stand for at least a couple of hours, then strain through cheesecloth into an airtight 1-pint glass container. Add the Cognac, orange flower water, and almond extract and stir. Seal the container and store in the refrigerator for up to 1 month.

SERVES

ONE

MALT FUJI

After winning the Chivas Master global cocktail competition, I was fortunate to travel with the brand and judge regional finals in many countries, including Japan. The best part was that I got to spend time with my good friend Max Warner, Chivas's global brand ambassador and an all-around awesome guy. When we were judging Japanese regional finals in Tokyo, I was asked to create a drink for the competing bartenders to enjoy. My inspiration came from two New York City bars. The first was Dante, with its take on the Garibaldi, a classic combination of Campari and ultra-fluffy orange juice. The second was the Horse's Apple at the now departed Suffolk Arms, with the guest's choice of spirit, freshly pressed Granny Smith apple juice and freshly grated horseradish. My creation marries Chivas 18 with "fluffy" Fuji apple juice. You can only get this texture using a Breville juicer (see page 56). Like a highball, it is an extremely simple drink, so texture, temperature, and perfect ingredients are paramount. The Chivas is beautiful, with its signature apple and stone fruit notes, with eighteen years describing the youngest whiskies in the blend that also contains much older ones. The fresh Fuji apple juice amplifies the sweetness of the malt and adds refreshing acidity as well. The buckwheat honey syrup gives roundness to the drink.

1¼ ounces Chivas Regal 18

¼ ounce Buckwheat Honey Syrup (recipe follows)

Fresh Fuji apple juice

Garnish: freshly grated cinnamon

Combine the whisky and honey syrup in a double old-fashioned glass over an ice sphere and top with apple juice. Garnish with freshly grated cinnamon.

BUCKWHEAT HONEY SYRUP
Makes 1½ cups

1 cup buckwheat honey
½ cup water

In a saucepan, combine the honey and water and heat over low heat, stirring to dissolve the honey. Transfer to an airtight 1-pint glass container. Seal the container and store in the refrigerator for up to 1 month

SERVES

ONE

ON APPLES AND BUCKWHEAT

Fuji apples are very meaningful to me on a personal level because they are widely cultivated in Nagano. Our family didn't have an apple orchard, but many folks around us did. In the countryside, everyone shares what they have. Our neighbors generously gifted apples to my grandma, who returned the favor with homemade mochi topped with a sauce made from hand-harvested walnuts. We always had apples in the house, especially during fall and winter. I'm sure they grew other varietals in Japan, but we grew up with Fuji apples, and that is what we knew. Nagano is also famous for its buckwheat crop and some of the best soba noodles in Japan. One of my favorite memories is taking my two grandmas out for lunch to our favorite soba restaurant in Minowa. Next to the cash register, they sold various buckwheat items, like soba tea. It's roasty and delicious. Buckwheat honey brings to mind this unique toasty aroma.

A SPECIAL GLASS

During one of my trips to Tokyo to attend the Japanese regional finals for Chivas Masters global cocktail competition, I had the opportunity to join a group of bartenders who were visiting Bar Time, a renowned bartending tools and glassware store. It is stocked top to bottom with amazing gear, and all the bartenders were wide-eyed, like kids in a candy store. The store's owner, Kenji Matsubuchi, asked me to prepare a cocktail using any tool or glass in the shop. Obviously, he had the whole setup and also keeps a nice supply of spirits and ice in his back office. I prepared an old-fashioned. I chose a stunning glass emblazoned with a 3D replica of Mount Fuji in its base, as well as a hand-etched mixing glass that was worthy of being displayed in a museum. Of course, I couldn't afford to purchase any of these treasures. A few months later, when I was behind the bar at Saxon + Parole, Mr. Matsubuchi walked into the bar and presented me with that very one-of-a-kind Mount Fuji glass, which he had hand-carried from Tokyo in a wooden box. He brought the exquisite mixing glass as well. I was moved beyond words, and this glass will always hold special meaning for me.

Combine the whiskey, syrup, lemon juice, corn puree, and crème fraîche in a cocktail shaker with ice. Shake and strain into an old-fashioned glass with fresh ice. Garnish with corn husks and crystallized soy sauce.

RECIPE
CONTINUES

Hokkaido is Japan's most northern island, a stone's throw from Russia, and is famous for its fertile land and seafood, several national parks, and ski resorts. But did you know it is also home to a beloved regional dish, miso butter corn ramen? Just like it sounds, it consists of your basic ramen noodles swimming in a miso broth that is enriched with corn kernels and a fat pat of butter that quickly melts and coats the entire surface. It is absolutely delicious, and I wanted to give a sense of it in a cocktail. I use Mellow Corn, a straight corn whiskey from Heaven Hill Distillery. The whiskey is fat-washed with butter to capture the round mouthfeel and give it a nuanced creamy flavor. White miso enters the picture, along with crème fraîche. Finally, I incorporate a corn puree made from rehydrated freeze-dried corn kernels. These have an intense corn flavor and allow for consistent results year-round. Of course, if it's the height of corn season, feel free to use a roasted sweet puree of fresh corn kernels instead.

2 ounces Salted Butter–Washed Whiskey (recipe follows)

¾ ounce Cornsilk Syrup (recipe follows)

¾ ounce fresh lemon juice

1 ounce Corn Puree (recipe follows)

1 barspoon White Miso–Crème Fraîche (recipe follows)

Garnish: corn husk and crystallized soy sauce

MISO BUTTERED CORN

SALTED BUTTER–WASHED WHISKEY

Makes 750ml

1½ ounces clarified salted butter

1 (750ml) bottle Mellow Corn whiskey, at room temperature

In a saucepan, heat the clarified butter over low heat to melt it completely. Pour the whiskey into an airtight 1-quart glass container and pour the clarified butter over the whiskey. Cover and let stand at room temperature for 1 hour, occasionally shaking the container. Store the mixture in the freezer overnight. The next day, strain the whiskey through cheesecloth to remove the butter solids. Pour the whiskey into its original bottle and store in the refrigerator for up to 2 months.

CORN SILK SYRUP

Makes 2 cups

1 cup dried corn silks

1 cup hot water

1 cup sugar

Steep the corn silks in the hot water for 5 minutes. Strain the water into an airtight 1-pint glass container to remove the cork silks, then add the sugar and stir well to dissolve. Seal the container and store in the refrigerator for up to 1 month.

WHITE MISO–CRÈME FRAÎCHE

Makes 1 cup

1 cup crème fraîche

1 tablespoon white miso paste

In a bowl, whisk together crème fraîche and miso. Transfer to an airtight glass 1-pint container. Seal the container and store in the refrigerator for up to 1 week.

CORN PUREE

Makes 1½ cups

2 cups freeze-dried corn kernels (see Note)

1 cup water

Soak the dried corn in the water to rehydrate. Transfer the mixture to a heavy-duty blender and puree. Pour into an airtight 1-pint glass container. Seal the container and store in the refrigerator for up to 3 days.

NOTE: *Fresh corn kernels can be used, if in season.*

This is my take on a classic Gin Daisy cocktail using *myoga,* a kind of Japanese ginger sprout with a distinctly refreshing flavor. My grandparents cultivated *myoga* in their garden, and every year, in the spring, it would shoot up flowering buds that we would harvest together, as needed. Traditionally, the buds, which are ruddy bronze on the outside and white within, are finely cut into slivers and are used as a condiment, adorning miso soup, soba noodles, and other dishes. It has a delicate, ginger-like spiciness. In this cocktail, fresh *myoga* gets muddled, and its herbaceous quality is ramped up with the addition of yellow Chartreuse, which is the defining modifier of the cocktail.

½ fresh myoga bud

¼ ounce simple syrup (page 56)

1½ ounces Suntory Roku gin

¾ ounce Combier liqueur

½ ounce fresh lemon juice

1 barspoon yellow Chartreuse

Pinch of salt

Splash of Champagne

Garnish: fresh myoga slice

Muddle the fresh myoga in a cocktail shaker with the simple syrup. Add the gin, Combier, lemon juice, Charteuse, and salt and shake with ice. Fine-strain into a tumbler and add a splash of Champagne. Fill the glass with crushed ice. Garnish with a slice of fresh myoga.

MYOGA FIX

SERVES

ONE

NO MAME WHEY

SERVES

ONE

Sometimes cocktails are inspired by savory dishes, and other times by desserts. This cocktail is a fun take on a margarita and takes its cues from a classic Japanese dessert called *zunda-mochi*. It is comprised of *mochi* (rice cakes) topped with savory and sweet edamame sauce. Most people are familiar with edamame steamed or boiled with sea salt that is served in restaurants and are surprised that the humble legume is also used in desserts. In *zunda,* the edamame are cooked with water, mashed, and sweetened to make a sauce. In this cocktail, the edamame forms the base of our silky pale green syrup. As the drink's foundation, I chose Milk-Washed Tequila, which adds a creamy, round mouthfeel and accounts for the "whey" in the drink's name. *Amazake,* a kind of no-alcohol sake, adds a hint of sweetness.

Lime Salt (recipe follows), for rimming the glass

Lime wedge, for rimming the glass

1½ ounce Milk-Washed Tequila (recipe follows)

½ ounce amazake (a kind of no-alcohol sake)

¾ ounce Zunda Syrup (recipe follows)

¾ ounce fresh lime juice

Garnish: pea shoot

Rim a quarter of a rocks glass with the lime salt (see page 55). Combine the tequila, amazake, syrup, and lime juice in a cocktail shaker with ice. Shake until chilled and fine-strain over fresh ice into a rocks glass. Garnish with a pea shoot.

MILK-WASHED TEQUILA

RECIPE ADAPTED FROM DON LEE OF EXISTING CONDITIONS

Makes about 1¼ quarts

1 (1L) bottle tequila

1 cup whole milk

½ ounce 10% citric acid solution

Combine the tequila and milk in a 2-quart glass container and stir well. Add the citric acid solution. Strain the mixture through cheesecloth and then through a coffee filter into an airtight 1½-quart glass container. Seal the container and store in the refrigerator for up to 2 weeks.

LIME SALT

Makes ½ cup

½ cup Maldon salt
Zest of 5 limes, grated on
a Microplane

Combine the salt and lime
zest in a mortar and grind
together using a pestle.
Transfer to an airtight
1-cup glass container.
Seal the container and
store in the pantry for up
to 1 week to maintain the
best color of the zest.

ZUNDA SYRUP

Makes 2 cups

1½ cups water
1¼ cups *wasanbon*
(premium fine-grained
Japanese cane sugar)
1 cup blanched shelled
edamame
¼ teaspoon citric acid

In a medium saucepan,
combine the water and
sugar and bring to a
simmer over medium
heat, stirring frequently
to dissolve the sugar.
Add the edamame and let
cool. Transfer the mixture
to a heavy-duty blender
and blend. Let rest for
at least 1 hour. Strain
through cheesecloth into
an airtight 1-pint glass
container. Add the citric
acid to help preserve the
vibrant color. Seal the
container and store in
the refrigerator for up
to 2 weeks.

SALTED SAKURA SYRUP

Makes 2 cups

1 tablespoon salted preserved sakura flower

1¼ cups water

1¼ cups sugar

1 barspoon Luxardo maraschino liqueur

Rinse the sakura flower in water to remove any excess salt and pat dry. In a small saucepan, combine the water and sakura flower and heat over medium-low heat. Add the sugar and stir to dissolve. Let cool, then strain through cheesecloth into an airtight 1-pint glass container. Stir in the maraschino liqueur. Seal the container and store in the refrigerator for up to 1 month.

The name of this cocktail refers to pineapple, the juice of which is prominently featured, and sensei (mentor), in this case, Naren Young, who introduced me to numerous classic cocktails. It is a cross between two historic drinks: the Algonquin, where the dry spice of rye whiskey is complemented by luscious fresh pineapple and herbaceous vermouth, and the East India Cocktail #2, with Cognac, fresh pineapple juice, orange curaçao, and maraschino liqueur. In this version, I use unaged, clear Armagnac, which conveys its vibrant grape base, as well as vermouth that features *sakura* (cherry blossoms) as one of its botanicals. I amp it up with Salted Sakura Syrup, which adds a touch of salinity.

1½ ounces Château de Pellehaut Blanche d'Armagnac

¾ ounce Mancino Sakura vermouth

1½ ounces fresh pineapple juice

½ ounce Salted Sakura Syrup (recipe at left)

¼ ounce Luxardo maraschino liqueur

Combine the armagnac, vermouth, pineapple juice, sakura syrup, and maraschino liqueur in a cocktail shaker with ice. Shake vigorously until chilled, then strain into a large coupe.

PINEAPPLE SENSEI

SERVES

ONE

SAKURA JULEP

As a huge fan of bourbon, I wanted to create a cocktail grounded in the classics that nods to Japan. This is a traditional Mint Julep variation. Peaches grow abundantly in the South, and are celebrated in many local drinks and dishes. Meanwhile, Nagano is famous for its stone fruits, including peaches (*momo*), plums, ume, and apricots. For this recipe, I use bourbon, a smidgen of peach liqueur, mint, and sugar. To this, I add an oleo-saccharum perfumed by preserved *sakura* (cherry blossom) leaves. They add a distinct herbaceousness and salinity that go well with the bourbon, and a touch of ginger acts as a bridge between the spirit and the peach flavor. Pro tip: Instead of muddling the mint leaves, rub them on the inside surface of the julep cup to really extract their fragrant essence.

SERVES

ONE

8 to 10 fresh mint leaves

2 ounces bourbon

¼ ounce peach liqueur

½ ounce Sakura Leaf Oleo-Saccharum (recipe follows)

1 barspoon Rich Ginger Syrup (recipe follows)

Garnish: mint sprig bouquet

Take the mint leaves, rub the inside of a julep cup, and leave them on the bottom. Add the bourbon, peach liqueur, oleo-saccharum, and syrup, fill the cup halfway with crushed ice, and stir to combine. Top off with more crushed ice and garnish with abundant sprigs of mint formed into a bouquet.

SAKURA LEAF OLEO-SACCHARUM

Makes 2 cups

1¾ cups sugar

Zest of 1 lemon, cut into strips with a peeler or paring knife

20 salted preserved sakura leaves

1 cup water

Combine the sugar, lemon zest, and sakura leaves in an airtight 1-pint glass container, cover and let stand at room temperature for 1 week. Add the water and stir to dissolve the sugar. Strain through cheesecloth into a clean 1-pint glass container. Seal the container and store in the refrigerator for up to 2 months.

RICH GINGER SYRUP

Make 2 cups

¾ cup cold-pressed fresh ginger juice

2¼ cups sugar

In an airtight 1-pint glass container, combine the ginger juice and the sugar and stir to dissolve the sugar. Seal the container and store in the refrigerator for up to 2 weeks.

TRUFFLE BUTTER–WASHED WHISKY

Makes 750ml

2 tablespoons clarified white truffle butter
1 (750ml) bottle Hibiki Japanese Harmony whisky

Combine the butter and whisky in an ROP bag and vacuum seal to remove all the air. Cook in a water bath using an immersion circulator at 135°F for 1 hour. Remove and let cool, then store in the freezer overnight. The next day, strain through cheesecloth into the original whisky bottle and store in the refrigerator for up to 1 month.

MATSUTAKE-PORCINI SYRUP

Makes 2 cups

1¼ cups water
½ cup dried matsutake mushrooms
¼ cup dried Italian porcini mushrooms
1¼ cups sugar

In a medium saucepan, bring the water to a simmer and add the dried mushrooms. Remove from the heat, cover, and steep for 15 minutes. Add the sugar to the liquid and stir to dissolve. Strain through cheesecloth into an airtight 1-pint glass container, squeezing the cheesecloth to extract all the liquid. Seal the container and store in the refrigerator for up to 2 weeks.

This cocktail is based on a drink that I made at Saxon + Parole, but I have tweaked it here by adding Japanese whisky and matsutake mushrooms. For the cocktail's foundation, I use Hibiki Japanese Harmony whisky, another beautiful expression from Suntory. It has elegant notes of oak and honey, which I thought would be nicely complemented by earthy mushrooms. I chose matsutake, a sought-after seasonal delicacy that grows at the feet of red pine trees and is incredibly fragrant. Many people compare them to porcinis. For this cocktail, I make a syrup that mixes these two exquisite mushrooms. To amplify the fungi quotient even further, I add the delectable flavor of truffles to the whisky and simply garnish the drink with a slice of Italian black truffle.

2 ounces Truffle Butter–Washed Whisky (recipe at left)

¼ ounce Matsutake-Porcini Syrup (recipe at left)

3 dashes chocolate bitters

Pinch of truffle salt

Garnish: freshly shaved black truffle slice

Combine the whisky, syrup, bitters, and truffle salt in a mixing glass with ice. Stir until chilled and strain into an old-fashioned glass over a large cube of ice. Garnish with a freshly shaved black truffle slice.

TRUFFLE OLD-FASHIONED

SERVES

ONE

SOME OF MY FAVORITE CREATIONS

165

UMESHU

SODA

SERVES

ONE

This drink makes use of umeshu, which many Japanese families prepare at home as part of a seasonal tradition, like my grandma did. Most commonly, umeshu's base is white liquor, which is basically a column still–produced shochu. This version is just like my grandma used to make, down to the exact proportions and techniques, but uses a Highland blanco tequila as a base. The spirit's tropical, fruity, and herbaceous notes nicely amplify the fresh aromatics of the ume without overpowering them. In a highball, this Nagano-meets-Jalisco mixture makes for a crushable summertime cooler, whether by the pool or on the edge of a rice paddy.

1¹/₂ ounces Homemade Umeshu (recipe follows)

Soda water, chilled

Garnish: lime twist

Pour the umeshu into a highball glass filled with ice. Top with chilled soda water and gently stir. Garnish with a lime twist.

HOMEMADE UMESHU

Makes 1 liter

2¼ cups fresh young green plums

1¾ cups rock sugar

1 (1L) bottle Olmeca Altos Plata tequila

Soak the plums in cold water to cover for 4 hours, then rinse each under running water and pat with a paper towel to dry completely. Create layers of alternating plums and rock sugar in an airtight 1½-quart glass container, then pour the tequila over the plums and sugar and seal the container tightly. Store in a dark, cool place for a minimum of 3 months to 1 year, shaking the container once in a while. Store in the pantry and it will age gracefully.

VALLEY STREAM

SERVES

SIX

TO

EIGHT

This is a punch that I created and have served at numerous charity events during my time in New York City. It is a crowd-pleaser that is ideal for parties and can be prepared ahead of time, with a big block of ice added just before serving. The inspiration here is the Bamboo cocktail, which is powered by dry vermouth and dry sherry. Bamboo is, of course, very Japanese and, growing up in a valley, the mountains behind our house were surrounded by stalks of wild bamboo. As a child, you learn how to fold bamboo leaves into little boats and then drop them in local streams, where you can follow them for miles. The drink's name pays homage to this memory.

3 tablespoons Lime Oleo-Saccharum (see page 123)

6 ounces fresh lime juice

6 ounces Bacardí Carta Blanca rum

2 ounces Noilly Prat extra dry vermouth

2 ounces Manzanilla sherry

2 ounces St-Germain elderflower liqueur

4 ounces Honeydew-Daiginjo Sherbet (recipe follows)

10 ounces cold brewed sencha green tea

Splash of dry sparkling wine

Garnish: cucumber slices, lime slices, bamboo leaves, and freshly grated nutmeg

In a punch bowl, dissolve the oleo-saccharum in the lime juice. Add the rum, vermouth, sherry, elderflower liqueur, sherbet, and tea along with a large block of ice. Top with a splash of dry sparkling wine. Garnish individual servings with cucumber and lime slices, bamboo leaves, and freshly grated nutmeg.

HONEYDEW-DAIGINJO SHERBET

Makes 2 cups

Zest of 3 limes, cut into strips with a peeler or paring knife

Peel of 1 cucumber

1¼ cups sugar

6 ounces fresh honeydew melon juice

2 ounces fresh cucumber juice

4 ounces junmai daiginjo sake

½ teaspoon citric acid

In a large bowl, muddle the lime zest and cucumber peels with the sugar. Cover and let stand for 30 minutes, then add the melon juice, cucumber, juice, sake, and citric acid and stir until the sugar has fully dissolved. Strain through cheesecloth into an airtight 1-pint glass container. Seal the container and store in the refrigerator for up to 2 days.

CHARCOAL-ROASTED BARLEY AND LAPSANG SOUCHONG TEA

Makes 1 quart

4 cups water

¼ cup charcoal-roasted mugicha (barley tea)

1½ teaspoons loose Lapsang Souchong tea leaves

Fill a 1-quart container with the water, add the teas, and let steep at room temperature for 30 minutes. Strain through a coffee filter into an airtight 1-quart glass container. Seal the container and store in the refrigerator for up to 3 days.

VANILLA SYRUP

Makes 2 cups

1¼ cups water

1¼ cups *sanonto* (Japanese light brown sugar), or light brown sugar

¼ vanilla bean

In a small saucepan, combine the water, sugar, and vanilla bean and bring to a simmer over medium-low heat, stirring until the sugar has dissolved. Remove from the heat and let stand for 30 minutes. Strain through cheesecloth into an airtight 1-pint glass container. Seal the container and store in the refrigerator for up to 1 month.

During the Meiji Dynasty and the Taishō era, Western culture, including its fashions, began filtering into the Japanese mainstream, with men's shirts featuring starched "high collars," which stood out in kimono-clad Japan. Over time, high collar, or *haikara* in Japanese, came to represent anything modern, Western, and trendy. My drink is a contemporary nonalcoholic version of an old-fashioned. This classic cocktail is traditionally whisk(e)y-based and in its place, I use charcoal-roasted barley tea, as malted barley is often part of a spirit's mash bill. This robustly flavored tea works as the structure of the drink, with Lapsang Souchong tea adding a peaty note. I add vanilla and bitters to simulate the effect of barrel aging.

3 ounces Charcoal-Roasted Barley and Lapsang Souchong Tea (recipe at left)

½ ounce Vanilla Syrup (recipe at left)

3 dashes Angostura bitters

Garnish: orange twist

Build the drink in a double rocks glass by adding the tea, syrup, and bitters over hand-carved ice. Stir until chilled. Garnish with an orange twist.

HAIKARA MUGICHA

SERVES

ONE

SOME OF MY FAVORITE CREATIONS

171

YUZU

HOPPY

SERVES

ONE

In the years following the end of World War II, many ordinary Japanese couldn't afford to enjoy beer on a daily basis. In its place was Hoppy, a nonalcoholic malt beverage, to which tipplers added their own spirit, like shochu, to obtain a "close enough" version of beer. Hoppy is seeing a revival today in Japan, as some believe it is healthier than regular beer, since it contains no purines, and shochu is considered a very clean distillate. While I won't venture a medical opinion, I'm a fan of Hoppy for its nostalgic taste. This is a nonalcoholic shandy with Hopped Yuzu Sherbet. Quaffable and sessionable, it showcases Cascade hops' refreshing nose, which pairs well with the uniquely zesty yuzu citrus.

¾ ounce Hopped Yuzu Sherbet (recipe follows)

1½ ounces water, chilled

Hoppy (or substitute any nonalcoholic beer), for topping

Garnish: yuzu wheel

Fill a collins glass with ice. Add the sherbet and water and stir until chilled. Top with Hoppy and gently stir. Garnish with a yuzu wheel.

HOPPED YUZU SHERBET
Makes 2 cups

Zest of 1 lemon, cut into strips with a peeler or paring knife

4 teaspoons Cascade hop pellets (available at homebrewing shops and online)

1¼ cups sugar

1 cup fresh lemon juice

¼ cup yuzu juice

In a bowl, muddle the lemon zest and hops with the sugar and let stand for 30 minutes. Add the lemon and yuzu juices and stir to dissolve the sugar. Strain through cheesecloth into an airtight 1-pint glass container. Seal the container and store in the refrigerator for up to 1 week.

5

MY FRIENDS

THE FOLLOWING ARE COCKTAILS FROM MY FRIENDS,
colleagues, teachers, and mentors, both in the US and in Japan.
Their thoughtful and delicious recipes highlight Japanese
ingredients and flavors and take their inspiration from a wide
array of sources: historical, literary, culinary, and even pop
culture.

SALTED LIME SYRUP
Makes 1 cup

1 cup water

1 cup sugar

Zest of 6 limes, cut into strips with a peeler or paring knife

1 tablespoon Maldon salt

In a small saucepan, combine the water and sugar and bring to a simmer over medium-high heat. Add the lime zest and salt, remove from the heat, and let cool. Strain into an airtight 1-cup glass container. Seal the container and store in the refrigerator for up to 1 month.

This cocktail is an Asian-inspired take on the gimlet, courtesy of Naren Young, formerly creative director of the highly acclaimed New York City restaurant bar Dante and its sister bar, Dante West Village. It is a study in simplicity, with bold fresh flavors and a hint of spice from wasabi. Naren, one of my esteemed sensei, splits the base down the middle between gin and shochu and creates his own cordial with housemade Salted Lime Syrup and yuzu juice. The gimlet originally has its roots in the British Navy, where a daily dose of lime juice was prescribed to prevent scurvy, and the enterprising sailors took it upon themselves to improve its flavor by mixing in their daily ration of gin.

1 ounce gin

1 ounce shochu

¾ ounce Salted Lime Syrup (recipe at left)

½ ounce yuzu juice

Pinch of wasabi powder or paste

½ teaspoon rice vinegar

Garnish: fresh shiso leaf

Combine the shochu, syrup, yuzu juice, wasabi powder or paste, and vinegar in a cocktail shaker with ice. Shake until chilled and double-strain into a frozen coupe. Garnish with a fresh shiso leaf.

NAREN YOUNG, BARTENDER,
NEW YORK, NEW YORK

FAR EAST GIMLET

SERVES

ONE

MY FRIENDS

FAR EAST SIDE

This fragrant and refreshing cocktail was created by my good friend, Kenta Goto, the owner of Bar Goto in New York City, Pegu Club alum, and winner of "American Bartender of the Year" at 2011 Tales of the Cocktail. The foundation of this cocktail is the Mojito, the famed Cuban cocktail redolent with rum and mint. A gin-based Mojito is called a Southside, so this cocktail, with a sake base, earns the clever moniker the Far East Side. The fact that it is sake-based lowers the ABV, with tequila acting in a supporting role.

3 fresh shiso leaves

2 ounces sake

¾ ounce elderflower liqueur

½ ounce tequila

¼ ounce fresh lemon juice

Garnish: fresh shiso leaf

Muddle the shiso leaves in a mixing glass. Add the sake, elderflower liqueur, tequila, and lemon juice with ice. Stir until chilled and strain into a Nick & Nora glass. Garnish with a fresh shiso leaf.

KENTA GOTO, BAR GOTO, NEW YORK, NEW YORK

MY FRIENDS

SERVES

ONE

A lower-ABV Manhattan was the inspiration for this cocktail by Natasha David, a Lower East Side bar luminary. Rather than a spirit foundation, it taps Japanese umeshu, a plum liqueur that, in this case, is made with sake rather than shochu, creating a less potent tipple. This note is further amplified by a splash of French plum brandy. Bourbon comes in as a modifier and gives this refined floral sipper a bit more of a backbone.

1½ ounces Kakurei junmai ginjo sake umeshu (or substitute another sake-based umeshu)

1½ ounces Cocchi Rosa

½ ounce Wild Turkey 101 bourbon

1 teaspoon Trimbach Mirabelle plum brandy

Garnish: brandied cherry

In a mixing glass, combine the sake, Cocchi Rosa, bourbon, and plum brandy with ice. Stir until chilled and strain into a Nick & Nora glass. Garnish with a brandied cherry.

NATASHA DAVID, NITECAP, NEW YORK, NEW YORK

ALWAYS FOREVER

SERVES

ONE

MY FRIENDS

ARIGATO SOUR

This drink was created by my good friend, the noted Sicilian-born bartender and former Palermo soccer star Salvatore Tafuri. Salvatore wanted to salute the sophistication and elegance of Japan's culture with a silky and balanced cocktail based on Japanese whisky, and I think he succeeded. The Arigato Sour's pink color and bracing *kabosu* citrus note make it a perfect aperitif cocktail.

1½ ounces Suntory Toki whisky

½ ounce Greenhook Ginsmiths beach plum gin liqueur

½ ounce St-Germain elderflower liqueur

1 ounce kabosu juice

½ ounce simple syrup (recipe on page 56)

1 ounce egg white

Garnish: edible blueberry-lemon sorbet violet flower (available online)

Combine the whisky, plum gin liqueur, elderflower liqueur, kabosu juice, simple syrup, and egg white in a cocktail shaker and dry shake without ice for 15 seconds. Add ice and shake for another 15 seconds, until chilled. Strain into a large coupe. Garnish with an edible flower, preferably a blueberry-lemon sorbet violet.

SALVATORE TAFURI, FORMERLY OF THE TIMES SQUARE EDITION, NEW YORK, NEW YORK

SERVES

ONE

IRI BANCHA–INFUSED JAPANESE WHISKY

Makes 750ml

1 (750ml) bottle Mars Whisky EXTRA Japanese whisky (or substitute Mars Iwai Tradition Japanese whisky)

3½ tablespoons loose iri bancha tea leaves

Combine the whisky and tea leaves in a 1-quart ROP bag and vacuum seal to remove all the air. Cook in a water bath using an immersion circulator at 122°F for 1 hour. Strain into the original whisky bottle and store in the pantry for up to 3 months.

HOJICHA–INFUSED CAMPARI

Makes 750ml

1 (750ml) bottle Campari

5 tablespoons loose hojicha tea leaves

Combine the Campari and tea leaves in a 1-quart ROP bag and vacuum seal to remove all the air. Cook in a water bath using an immersion circulator at 122°F for 1 hour. Strain into the original Campari bottle and store in the pantry for up to 3 months.

SHINYA SAKURAI, SAKURAI JAPANESE TEA EXPERIENCE, TOKYO, JAPAN

Shinya Sakurai, a former bartender who became a Master of Tea, opened Sakurai Japanese Tea Experience in Tokyo with the mission to educate Japan's next generation about the beauty of this beverage and its healthful properties. In this cocktail, Shinya wants to celebrate *nigami*, which refers to the pleasingly bitter element found in tea that is beloved by Japanese. By infusing Campari with roasted green tea, he transforms a traditional Western bitter liqueur into a distinctly Japanese one.

1½ ounces Iri Bancha–Infused Japanese Whisky (recipe at left)

⅔ ounce Hojicha-Infused Campari (recipe at left)

⅔ ounce Carpano Antica Formula vermouth

Garnish: torched dehydrated orange slice

Build the drink by adding the whisky, Campari, and vermouth to an old-fashioned glass over ice. Stir until chilled. Garnish with a torched dehydrated orange slice.

BANCHA NEGRONI

SERVES

ONE

MY FRIENDS

SALINE SOLUTION

Makes ½ cup

½ cup water

1 tablespoon salt, any kind

Combine the water and salt in a 4-ounce atomizer spray bottle. Shake until the salt has dissolved completely and store in the refrigerator for up to 1 month.

For this cocktail, world-renowned Japanese bartender and bar owner Shingo Gokan, the force behind The SG Club in Tokyo and Shanghai's Speak Low, Sober Company, and the Odd Couple, took as his inspiration the Hinomaru bento box. Consisting of simple and humble white rice crowned with a single umeboshi (pickled plum) placed in the center, it represents the ultimate minimalist presentation and also suggests the Japanese flag with the red circle on a white background. To construct the drink, Shingo turns to a rice shochu to represent the white of the flag and a single ume to symbolize the rising sun. He adds a touch of umeshu (plum liqueur) and a spray of saline to re-create the sensation of the umeboshi.

1 ounce The SG Club Kome shochu (or substitute any rice shochu)

1 ounce umeshu (plum liqueur)

1 dash Peychaud's bitters

2 dashes rice vinegar

Garnish: 2 sprays Saline Solution (recipe at left) and a crunchy ume

Combine the shochu, umeshu, bitters, and vinegar in a mixing glass with ice. Stir until chilled and strain over hand-carved ice in an old-fashioned glass. Apply 2 sprays of saline solution and garnish with a crunchy ume.

SHINGO GOKAN, THE SG CLUB, TOKYO, JAPAN

BENTO ON THE ROCK

SERVES ONE

MY FRIENDS

BUBBLE FICTION

This pop culture–inspired cocktail comes courtesy of Lynnette Marrero, beverage director of Llama San, a New York City restaurant celebrating Peru's Nikkei cuisine that incorporates Japanese foodways. It takes its name from the movie *Bubble Fiction: Boom or Bust,* where Mayumi, a bar hostess, returns to 1990 via a time-traveling washing machine in an attempt to prevent Japan's "bubble" economy from bursting. The cocktail is a twist on the classic beer-based shandy.

½ ounce Rich Ginger Syrup (page 162)

½ ounce Yuzuri liqueur (or substitute a yuzu liqueur)

½ ounce fresh lemon juice

¼ ounce yuzu juice

Hitachino Nest Weizen (or substitute any hefeweizen beer)

Garnish: an ornate lemon garnish

Combine the syrup, Yuzuri, lemon juice, and yuzu juice in a mixing glass with ice. Gently stir and strain into a pint glass. Add ice, top with the beer, and gently stir again. Top with an ornate lemon garnish.

LYNNETTE MARRERO, LLAMA SAN, NEW YORK, NEW YORK

SERVES

O N E

CAT'S PAW

SERVES

ONE

This cocktail, a twist on the Red Hook, which is itself a Brooklyn variation of the classic Manhattan, was created by Erick Castro, the renowned West Coast bar star. In his drink, sesame-infused Japanese whisky takes the place of rye, with ginger liqueur and Marsala wine replacing maraschino liqueur and Punt e Mes. Its feline name is rooted in history and politics, of which Erick is a keen student. He's long been fascinated with samurai, Japan's feudal military caste that was governed by Bushido (the Way of the Warrior), a code that prized honor and loyalty, and dictated nearly all areas of a samurai's life. During times of political intrigue or upheaval, it would sometimes be necessary to engage in clandestine techniques and tactics, such as spying, espionage, and assassinations. However, this behavior was seen as contravening Bushido. A practical workaround was that the *katana*-wielding samurai would use ninjas (mercenary martial artists and saboteurs) as their proxies to do their bidding. Since ninjas were typically of a lower caste than samurai and not held to the standards of Bushido, these "dishonorable" tactics could be employed without fear of shame. Having others do one's dirty work, as a cat's paw does for the cat, goes back, no doubt, to the beginning of time, and there is no shortage of it today.

1½ ounces Sesame Oil-Washed Japanese Whisky (recipe follows)

¾ ounce ginger liqueur

¾ ounce Madeira wine (or substitute Carpano Antica Formula vermouth)

2 drops Kishibori Shoyu barrel-aged soy sauce (available in Japanese markets and online)

Garnish: 1 by 3-inch rectangle nori

Combine the whisky, ginger liqueur, Madeira, and soy sauce in a mixing glass with ice. Stir until chilled and pour into a soy sauce serving vessel. To serve, pour the contents over a large cube of ice in an old-fashioned glass. Garnish with a nori rectangle sitting atop the rim of the glass.

ERICK CASTRO, RAISED BY WOLVES AND POLITE PROVISIONS, SAN DIEGO, CALIFORNIA

SESAME OIL–WASHED JAPANESE WHISKY

Makes 1 liter

1 (1L) bottle Suntory Toki whisky

½ cup high-quality sesame oil

Combine the whisky and oil in a 1½-quart ROP bag. Vacuum seal to remove all the air. Cook in a water bath using an immersion circulator at 135°F for 2 hours. Cool the bag in the freezer, then strain the mixture through cheesecloth into the original whisky bottle and store in the refrigerator for up to 1 month.

DAIKON

PALOMA

This spin on a Paloma was created by Hiroyasu Kayama, owner of Bar Ben Fiddich, an acclaimed cocktail bar in Tokyo that specializes in innovative farm-to-glass cocktails, with fresh ingredients harvested on his family's nearby farm. The bar's shelves are bedecked with glass jars containing various experimental infusions and tinctures. The unexpected element in this Paloma variation is daikon, a large radish that is a key vegetable in traditional Japanese cuisine. But Hiroyasu breaks new ground by applying its juice in a refreshing and satisfying way.

Salt, for rimming the glass

Lime wedge, for rimming the glass

1½ ounces tequila

2 ounces daikon juice (see Note)

⅓ ounce fresh lime juice

Tonic water

Garnish: daikon slices

Rim a cocktail tumbler with salt (see page 55). Place a large cube of ice in the glass and add the tequila, daikon juice, and lime juice. Stir until chilled and top with tonic water. Garnish with daikon slices.

NOTE: *To prepare fresh daikon juice, process a peeled daikon radish in a slow-speed juicer to preserve its delicate, fragrant aroma.*

HIROYASU KAYAMA, BAR BEN FIDDICH, TOKYO, JAPAN

SERVES

O N E .

DASHI PAPI

This drink is the brainchild of Gabe Orta, founder and operator of the high-energy Broken Shaker bars and Bar Lab, a cocktail consultancy firm. Gabe named it after his alter ego's nickname, which he earned by always making dashi at home and cooking Asian ingredients with Latin flavors. In his margarita variation, kombu-infused tequila adds a subtle umami component to the drink, while the rice syrup imparts texture and, with an aromatic mezcal liqueur, balances the zestiness of the fresh lemon juice.

Togarashi Salt (recipe follows), for rimming the glass

Lemon wedge, for rimming the glass

1 ounce Kombu-Infused Tequila (recipe follows)

½ ounce Del Maguey Crema de Mezcal liqueur

¾ ounce Rice Syrup (recipe follows)

1 ounce fresh lemon juice

Rim half a rocks glass filled with ice with togarashi salt (see page 55). Combine the tequila, mezcal liqueur, rice syrup, and lemon juice in a cocktail shaker with ice. Shake until chilled and strain into the prepared rocks glass.

GABE ORTA, BROKEN SHAKER, MIAMI, LOS ANGELES, CHICAGO, AND NEW YORK

TOGARASHI SALT
Makes 1½ cups

1 cup sea salt
½ cup togarashi

Combine the salt and togarashi in an airtight 1-pint glass container. Seal the container and store in the pantry for up to 1 year.

KOMBU-INFUSED TEQUILA
Makes 750ml

1 (750ml) bottle silver tequila (preferably from the Highlands)
1 sheet kombu, rinsed in water

Warm the tequila by heating it in the microwave for 30 seconds or gently warming it in a saucepan on the stovetop over medium-low heat for 3 minutes. Remove from the heat, combine with kombu in an airtight 1-quart glass container, cover and let stand for 3 hours. Strain into the original tequila bottle and store in the refrigerator for up to 6 months.

RICE SYRUP

Makes 1 cup

1 cup uncooked white rice
1 cup water
1 cup sugar

In a large pot, combine the rice and water and bring to a rolling boil over medium-high heat. Strain the water (discarding the rice) and return it to the pot. Add the sugar, reduce the heat to medium-low and simmer for about 2 minutes, stirring until the sugar has fully dissolved. Let cool, then transfer to an airtight 1-cup glass container. Seal the container and store in the refrigerator for up to 2 weeks.

GINZA STAR

1½ ounces Hibiki
Japanese Harmony
whisky

1 ounce Kamoizumi
red maple sake (or
substitute a medium-
bodied sake)

¼ ounce Drambuie

1 dash Angostura
Bitters

1 dash shio koji
(available at
Japanese markets and
online)

Garnish: star-shaped
orange disc

Combine the whisky,
sake, Drambuie,
bitters, and shio koji
in a mixing glass with
ice. Stir until chilled
and strain into a chilled
coupe. Garnish with
a star-shaped orange
disc.

*JEFF BELL, PDT (PLEASE
DON'T TELL), NEW YORK AND
HONG KONG*

This cocktail was contributed by Jeff Bell, bar director of PDT, who earned "American Bartender of the Year" at 2017 Tales of the Cocktail and is a co-consulting master blender of Bertoux brandy. An elegant and handsome sipper, it is a Manhattan-style cocktail made with predominantly Japanese ingredients. There is a series of variations of this cocktail that are named for different parts of New York City, like Brooklyn, Little Italy, Bensonhurst, Greenpoint, and others. This Japan-centric variation is named for the Ginza district in Tokyo, where Jeff had his first introduction to the Japanese cocktail scene at the renowned Bar High Five and Star Bar. The cocktail employs Japanese whisky instead of the traditional bourbon or rye and swaps in sake and Drambuie for sweet vermouth. The sake is rather unique. It is a *namazake,* meaning it is unpasteurized, preserving its fresh flavors. But what sets this sake apart is that it is then aged for two years at a temperature near freezing. The resulting liquid is somewhat reminiscent of port wine or sherry. A bit of *shio koji,* a traditional Japanese seasoning, elevates the drink's umami quotient.

SERVES

ONE

MY FRIENDS

197

GODZILLA

Globetrotting bar legend Nico de Soto, a close friend, has traveled to more of the world's top bars than anyone else I know. For his creative interpretation of a classic Flip, he looked to the giant green monster of Japanese science fiction movies. The cocktail's emerald hue is a suitable salute to the radioactive creature, and its ease of drinking perhaps highlights Godzilla's softer side, when on breaks from attacking Tokyo or tussling with other *kaiju*. It uses three key Japanese ingredients: rice milk, *anko* (sweetened red bean paste), and matcha.

¾ ounce rye whiskey

¾ ounce cream sherry

1½ ounces Matcha Anko Rice Milk Syrup (recipe follows)

1 whole egg

Garnish: Takesumi bamboo salt and crumbled matcha Kit Kats

Combine the whiskey, sherry, rice milk syrup, and egg in a cocktail shaker and dry shake without ice for 12 seconds. Add ice, shake for another 12 seconds, then double-strain into a sake glass. Garnish with Takesumi bamboo salt and crumbled matcha Kit Kats.

NICO DE SOTO, DANICO, PARIS; KAIDO, MIAMI; AND MACE, NEW YORK

MATCHA ANKO RICE MILK SYRUP
Makes 1¼ quarts

4 cups water

¾ cup rice

4 cups sugar

2 tablespoons matcha powder

1½ tablespoons anko (sweetened red bean paste)

1 dash rye whiskey

Combine the water and rice in a blender and puree. Double-strain into a 1½-quart container. Add the sugar and stir to dissolve. Add the matcha and anko and stir until incorporated. Add a dash of rye whiskey as a preservative. Seal the container and store in the refrigerator for up to 5 days.

SERVES

ONE

GYMKHANA

This cocktail came to life behind the bar at the high-energy contemporary Indian restaurant GupShup, located in Manhattan's Gramercy Park neighborhood. Created by bartender Mikey Belasco, its name is Hindi for a social club where members traditionally gather to *gupshup* ("gossip" in Hindi) and enjoy time away from home. Mikey wanted to create a drink that honors Japanese spirits, including rice-based vodka and two kinds of shochu, one at a traditional proof of 25% ABV and a higher one at 43% ABV to maximize the barley flavor notes. The mixture adds a different layer to the cocktail and complements the vodka. A small touch of Campari lends a little extra bitter note while adding color to complement the sweet and tart flavors of raspberry.

In a cocktail shaker, muddle the raspberries. Add the vodka, shochus, Campari, vermouth, lemon juice, simple syrup, and bitters with ice and shake until chilled. Strain into a collins glass over fresh ice and top with ginger beer. Garnish with a lemon wheel and a pineapple leaf.

MIKEY BELASCO, GUPSHUP, NEW YORK, NEW YORK

MY FRIENDS

SERVES

ONE

3 raspberries

¾ ounce Suntory Haku vodka

¼ ounce iichiko Saiten shochu

¼ ounce iichiko Silhouette shochu

¼ ounce Campari

¼ ounce sweet vermouth

¾ ounce fresh lemon juice

½ ounce simple syrup (see page 56)

2 dashes Angostura bitters

Ginger beer

Garnish: lemon wheel and pineapple leaf

HATTORI HANZO

SERVES

ONE

This cocktail takes its name from the legendary katana-wielding samurai Hattori Hanzo, whose name was memorialized by Quentin Tarantino in *Kill Bill*. Its creator, Gates Otsuji, is the founder of Controlled Substances, a cocktail and beverage consultancy, and this martini variation exudes a wealth of subtle, delicately nuanced flavors. Gates's inspiration was his Japanese grandmother's *goma* (sesame) pickles, which were present at every family gathering. Here they are incorporated both in the glass and as a garnish. In this cocktail, he calls for "Mirror of Truth," a lovely sake that dances gently across the palate, with a subtle grassy note to complement the fragrant botanicals of Beefeater 24 gin, especially Japanese sencha. The kombu, added to the pickling brine, provides enough umami to give heft to the cocktail and round out the edges on the palate.

2 Fresno chile slices

1 drop sriracha (optional)

2 ounces Beefeater 24 gin

1 ounce Masumi Okuden Kantsukuri "Mirror of Truth" junmai sake

½ ounce Dolin dry vermouth (or substitute Noilly Prat vermouth)

½ ounce Goma Pickle Brine (recipe follows)

1 dash bergamot citrus puree (preferably Boiron)

Garnish: slice of Goma Pickle (recipe follows)

Gently crush the Fresno chile slices in a mixing glass and add a drop of sriracha, if desired. Add the gin, sake, vermouth, brine, and citrus puree and fill the glass with ice. Stir the drink to chill and fine-strain into a chilled cocktail glass. Garnish with a goma pickle slice.

GATES OTSUJI, CONTROLLED SUBSTANCES, NEW YORK NEW YORK

GOMA PICKLE SLICES

Makes 1 cup

1½ cups Japanese rice vinegar

½ cup sugar

½ teaspoon kosher salt

Kombu (dried Japanese kelp), to taste

½ teaspoon sesame seeds

2 Kirby cucumbers, sliced into thin rounds

In a small saucepan, whisk together the vinegar, sugar, and salt. Add thin strips of kombu to the liquid to taste and bring the mixture to a low simmer over medium heat. Remove from the heat and let cool. Pour the liquid into an airtight 1-pint glass container and refrigerate until chilled. Toast the sesame seeds in a dry pan over medium heat until browned and aromatic. Transfer the toasted seeds to the chilled pickling liquid and add the cucumbers. Seal the container and agitate gently to coat the cucumber slices with the brine. Return the container to the refrigerator for 1 to 3 hours before using. The cucumbers will keep for about 1 week and the brine can be reused for up to 1 week. (Note: Whole cucumbers can also be pickled; submerge in the liquid, weighting the cucumbers as necessary to keep them below the liquid, and pickle for 36 to 72 hours.)

SHISO SYRUP

Makes 2 cups

1¼ cups sugar
1¼ cups water
20 fresh shiso leaves

In a small saucepan, combine the sugar and water and bring to a boil over medium-high heat, stirring to dissolve the sugar. Remove the pot from the heat, add the shiso leaves, cover, and steep for 20 minutes. Strain into an airtight 1-pint glass container. Seal the container and store in the refrigerator for up to 2 weeks.

This drink was created by my dear comrade in arms, Nacho, creative director at Ghost Donkey. Highland refers here to the landscape of Jalisco, which is one of the most important tequila-producing regions in Mexico. I've learned so much from Nacho over the years and, in turn, was privileged to introduce him to Japanese ingredients, like yuzu and shiso, which are celebrated in this drink.

1 ounce Montelobos mezcal

1 ounce Olmeca Altos Plata tequila

½ ounce yuzu juice

½ ounce fresh lime juice

½ ounce Shiso Syrup (recipe at left)

½ ounce agave syrup (1:1 agave nectar to water)

1 egg white

Garnish: yukari and half of a dehydrated orange wheel

Combine the mezcal, tequila, yuzu juice, lime juice, shiso syrup, agave syrup, and egg white in a cocktail shaker and dry shake without ice. Add ice and shake until chilled, then strain into a large coupe. Garnish with a sprinkle of yukari on the top and half of a dehydrated orange wheel.

IGNACIO "NACHO" JIMENEZ, GHOST DONKEY, NEW YORK, NEW YORK

HIGHLAND PICNIC

SERVES

ONE

MY FRIENDS

205

JAZZ LINGO

SERVES

ONE

Brian Evans, Bar Director at Sunday in Brooklyn in Williamsburg, Brooklyn, created this earthy and grassy gin fizz variation, thanks to matcha. Its name is a nod to Japan's infatuation with jazz music. The love affair started back in the early twentieth century, when Japanese musicians, who played on ocean liners docked in the US, went offshore and were exposed to the music, which they brought back to Japan. After World War II, jazz musicians were in high demand at US Army base officers' clubs. From there, jazz went mainstream and was widely embraced.

¾ ounce Bols genever

¾ ounce Fords gin

½ ounce Lustau Vermut Blanco

¾ ounce Pistachio Orgeat (recipe follows, or use BG Reynolds or Small Hands almond orgeat)

½ ounce fresh lemon juice

¾ ounce egg white

1 barspoon matcha

Soda water, chilled

Garnish: 1 matcha-flavored Pocky stick

Combine the genever, gin, Lustau, orgeat, lemon juice, egg white, and matcha in a cocktail shaker and dry-shake without ice for 10 seconds. Add 3 ice cubes and shake for 3 seconds. Double-strain into a chilled collins glass over fresh ice. Allow the foam to settle a bit, then top with chilled soda water. Garnish with a matcha-flavored Pocky stick on top.

BRIAN EVANS, SUNDAY IN BROOKLYN, BROOKLYN, NEW YORK

PISTACHIO ORGEAT
Makes 3 cups

¾ cup shelled pistachios

2½ cups hot water (not boiling)

2 cups sugar

1 ounce vodka

Preheat the oven to 300°F. Spread the nuts over a baking sheet and toast in the oven for about 4 minutes. Transfer the nuts to a heavy-duty blender, add the hot water, and blend on high for 1 minute. Strain the nut milk through a fine-mesh strainer or cheesecloth and return it to the blender. Add the sugar and vodka and blend again. Pour into an airtight 1-quart glass container. Seal the container and store in the refrigerator for up to 1 month.

LEMONGRASS SYRUP

Makes 1 cup

10 lemongrass stalks, ends trimmed and brittle outer layers removed

2 cups water

1 cup sugar

Puree the lemongrass in a food processor and transfer to a saucepan. Add the water and simmer over medium heat until the mixture has reduced by half, about 40 minutes. Remove from the heat and let cool. Transfer to an airtight 1-cup glass container, cover and refrigerate overnight. The next morning, strain the lemongrass mixture through a fine-mesh sieve into a bowl and discard the lemongrass pulp. Measure the infused water and pour it into a saucepan. Add an equal amount of granulated sugar (it should be about 1 cup) and cook over medium heat, stirring, until the sugar has dissolved, 3 to 5 minutes. Remove the pan from heat and let cool completely. Pour the syrup into an airtight 1-cup glass container. Seal the container and store in the refrigerator for up to 2 weeks.

This cocktail is by Julie Reiner, a leading light of the cocktail renaissance, whose Flatiron Lounge proved that excellent craft cocktails could be made in high volume. She brought craft cocktails to Brooklyn with Clover Club, and her nearby bar, Leyenda, celebrates Latin spirits. Julie grew up on Oahu in Hawaii, and her family had a lychee tree in their front yard. She devoured fresh lychees all the time and wanted to use them in a cocktail. Julie created this libation, as well as a zero-proof version of the drink (without the gin) and named it after her daughter, whose middle name is Leilani, Hawaiian for "heavenly flower." Her little girl adores the taste of lychees and really enjoys the nonalcoholic version of this drink.

2 lychee nuts, peeled and pitted

2 ounces Ki No Bi Kyoto dry gin (or substitute Tanqueray, Fords, or Plymouth gin)

½ ounce fresh lime juice

¾ ounce Lemongrass Syrup (recipe at left)

½ ounce lychee juice

Soda water, chilled

Garnish: lemongrass stalk and lime wheel

Muddle the lychee fruit in a cocktail shaker. Add the gin, lime juice, lemongrass syrup, lychee juice, and ice. Shake until chilled, strain into a chilled collins glass over fresh ice, and top with chilled soda water. Garnish with a lemongrass stalk and a lime wheel.

JULIE REINER, CLOVER CLUB AND LEYENDA, BROOKLYN, NEW YORK

LEILANI'S FIZZ

SERVES ONE

MY FRIENDS

209

A LETTER FROM THE SHOGUN

SERVES

ONE

This recipe is from one of my first bartending mentors, Yasuyuki "Antonio" Suzuki of Tableaux Lounge in Tokyo, under whose tutelage I spent many of my formative years. Antonio's inspiration harkens back to the historic Battle of Yamazaki, waged in 1582 in present-day Kyoto. The letter in question was from Akechi Mitsuhide, a renegade samurai who had killed his own warlord, Oda Nobunaga, and usurped his power. Compounding this ultimate betrayal, the letter was an appeal to a rival clan to help Mitsuhide consolidate his ill-gotten gains. Forces loyal to the rightful heir, Toyotomi Hideyoshi, intercepted the letter and subsequently defeated the rogue samurai. Hideyoshi went on to become one of Japan's great unifiers. Antonio's choice of Yamazaki whisky pays tribute to this battle, with strawberry and pomegranate adding seasonal acidity. It celebrates the triumph of honor and fealty over arrogance and greed.

1½ ounces Strawberry and Pomegranate-Infused Japanese Whisky (recipe follows)

⅓ ounce sake-based yuzu liqueur

¼ ounce fresh lime juice

1 barspoon grenadine

Garnish: Japanese *momiji* (maple) leaf

Combine the whisky, yuzu liqueur, lime juice, and grenadine in a cocktail shaker with ice. Shake until chilled and strain into a Japanese matcha tea cup over a large piece of hand-carved ice. Garnish with a Japanese momiji (maple) leaf.

STRAWBERRY AND POMEGRANATE-INFUSED JAPANESE WHISKY

Makes 750mL

1 (750mL) bottle Yamazaki Japanese whisky (or substitute Yamazaki 12-year-old Japanese whisky)

6 strawberries

Seeds of ¼ whole pomegranate

Combine the whisky, strawberries, and pomegranate seeds in an airtight 1-quart glass container, cover and let stand at room temperature for 14 to 21 days. Once the color of the fruit has permeated the liquid, strain it into the original whisky bottle and store in the refrigerator for up to 1 month.

YASUYUKI "ANTONIO" SUZUKI, TABLEAUX LOUNGE, TOKYO, JAPAN

LOCAL WHISKY BLEND

Makes 3 cups

1 cup Nikka Taketsuru Pure Malt whisky

1 cup Nikka Black Deep Blend whisky

1 cup Nikka Black Rich Blend whisky

Combine the whiskies in an airtight 1-quart glass container. Seal the container and store in the pantry indefinitely.

Necessity is the mother of invention, and this cocktail came about as the result of the skyrocketing prices of Japanese whisky in Japan. Hisashi Watanabe, bartender and owner of Bar Gyu+ in Hokkaido, Japan, still wanted to use his country's renowned whisky in cocktails, but its prospects were looking grim. Undeterred, Hisashi sent his team out to buy up all the affordable whiskies and proceeded to create a house blend of three whiskies from Nikka—Taketsuru Pure Malt, Black Deep Blend, and Black Rich Blend—that wouldn't break the bank. Taketsuru Pure Malt is a no-age statement blended malt whisky (said to be ten years old) named after Nikka's founder, and is the company's respected entry-level pour. The blend contains whiskies from their Miyagikyo and Yoichi distilleries, including sherry cask–finished malts, which impart richness. A simple old-fashioned is the best way to showcase this clever concoction's multilayered complexity.

3 brown sugar cubes

2 dashes Angostura bitters

2 ounces Local Whisky Blend (recipe at left)

Garnish: orange twist

In an old-fashioned glass, muddle the sugar cubes and bitters. Add the whisky and a large cube of ice and stir until the sugar has dissolved and the drink is chilled. Express an orange twist and place it in the cocktail.

HISASHI WATANABE, BAR GYU+, HOKKAIDO, JAPAN

LOCAL WHISKY OLD-FASHIONED

SERVES

ONE

MY FRIENDS

ODANGO

Bartender Toshihiro Fukami took inspiration from *dango,* a traditional Japanese treat made from *mochiko* (rice flour) that is formed into little spheres, which are then skewered. It is related to *mochi,* Japanese rice flour sweets. In his home prefecture of Kumamoto, the tasty buns are called *ikinari dango* and are stuffed with *anko* (sweetened red bean paste) and sweet potatoes. This drink is a twist on the classic Alexander and swaps in a barrel-aged rice shochu for the traditional brandy, as well as providing a jolt from coffee liqueur.

1½ ounces Hakutake Kin Shiro rice shochu

⅓ ounce Mr. Black coffee liqueur

⅓ ounce anko (sweetened red bean paste)

1 ounce heavy cream

⅓ ounce simple syrup (see page 56)

1 dash Angostura bitters

Garnish: ground coffee and sweet potato chips

Combine the shochu, coffee liqueur, anko, cream, simple syrup, and bitters in a cocktail shaker with ice. Shake until chilled and strain into a coupe. Garnish with a sprinkling of ground coffee and sweet potato chips.

TOSHIHIRO FUKAMI, HUGE CO. LTD., TOKYO, JAPAN

SERVES

ONE

PACIFIC 75

This French 75 variation was created by Lucas Swallows, bar director of Momofuku, chef David Chang's highly influential Asian-inflected restaurant empire that started in the East Village and is now a trendsetting powerhouse. The elegant sipper was designed for Majordomo, the group's Los Angeles restaurant, and showcases aromatic spirits and modifiers spanning and connecting the Land of the Rising Sun with the Golden State. The cocktail splits the base between the traditional gin, here Japanese, and a citrusy yuzu sake. California sparkling wine and honey bring the West Coast influence.

3 ounces California brut sparkling wine (bottles by Cruse Wine Co. are worth considering, as are other bottle-conditioned sparklers)

¾ ounce Ki No Bi Kyoto dry gin (or substitute Suntory Roku gin)

1¾ ounces Joto yuzu sake

¼ ounce California acacia honey syrup (see note)

½ ounce fresh lemon juice

Pour the sparkling wine into a chilled Champagne flute. Combine the gin, sake, honey syrup, and lemon juice in a cocktail shaker with ice. Shake until chilled and strain into the flute with the sparkling wine.

NOTE: *To make this syrup, mix ¾ teaspoon honey with ¾ teaspoon water.*

LUCAS SWALLOWS, MAJORDOMO, LOS ANGELES, CALIFORNIA

SERVES

O N E

ASIAN CITRUS BLEND

Makes 1 cup

4 ounces fresh lemon juice

3 ounces fresh Mandarin orange juice

1 ounce yuzu juice

Combine the juices in an airtight 1-cup glass container. Seal the container and store in the refrigerator for up to 3 days.

BURDOCK ROOT TINCTURE

Makes 1 cup

1 (4-inch) piece burdock root, peeled and chopped

1 cup Everclear or high-proof vodka

Place the chopped burdock root and Everclear in an airtight 1-cup glass container. Cover and let stand at room temperature for 48 hours, then strain into a clean 1-cup glass container. Seal the container and store in the pantry for up to 3 months.

While popular songs and books are common sources of inspiration for cocktail names, this one celebrates origami, the Japanese art of creating intricate sculptures by artfully folding paper. Caer Maiko, bartender at the Roosevelt Room in Austin, Texas, and co-founder of Daijoubu Pop Up, developed this cocktail as an homage to the origami cranes, which almost every Japanese person masters. It is an Asian-accented riff on the Paper Plane, a contemporary classic cocktail that Sam Ross made for the Violet Hour in Chicago, which is itself a twist on the Last Word, a revered classic cocktail. So this is a twist on a twist of a classic drink, which demonstrates how bartenders respect their forerunners, yet feel free to improvise and innovate.

¾ ounce Suntory Toki whisky

¾ ounce Asian Citrus Blend (recipe at left)

½ ounce Amaro Nonino

½ ounce Aperol

½ ounce Tempus Fugit crème de banane

1 dash Burdock Root Tincture (recipe at left)

Garnish: 3 drops sesame oil and an origami paper crane

Combine the whisky, citrus blend, Amaro Nonino, Aperol, crème de banane, and tincture in a cocktail shaker with ice. Shake and strain into a chilled coupe. Garnish with 3 drops of sesame oil on the surface and an origami paper crane clipped to the stem of the glass.

CAER MAIKO, THE ROOSEVELT ROOM, AUSTIN, TEXAS

PAPER CRANE

SERVES

ONE

MY FRIENDS

SAGE THE WORLD

SERVES

ONE

A play on the phrase "Save the World," this drink was created by Soran Nomura, former bar manager of Fuglen Tokyo and a bartender at Guzzle at the SG Club in Tokyo. It commemorates Jiro Shirasu, a Japanese economist who promoted a close relationship between Japan and the US following World War II, thereby safeguarding peace and, in a way, saving the world from future destruction. Sage and green tea definitely lend a fragrant Japanese note to this Last Word variation, which also includes gin, sherry, and lemon juice.

Absinthe (for spritzing)

2 fresh sage leaves

1 ounce G'Vine Nouaison gin

¾ ounce Manzanilla sherry

⅔ ounce fresh lemon juice

½ ounce Sage and Green Tea Syrup (recipe follows)

Garnish: fresh sage leaf

Spray the inside of a coupe with absinthe. In a cocktail shaker, muddle the sage leaves. Add the gin, sherry, lemon juice, and syrup with ice and shake until chilled. Double-strain into the prepared coupe. Garnish with a fresh sage leaf.

SORAN NOMURA, GUZZLE AT THE SG CLUB, TOKYO, JAPAN

SAGE AND GREEN TEA SYRUP
Makes 2 cups

1¼ cups water

1¼ cups sugar

7 fresh sage leaves

2 teaspoons loose green tea leaves

In a small saucepan, combine the water and sugar and bring to a slow simmer over medium-high heat, stirring until the sugar has dissolved. Remove from the heat and add the sage leaves and green tea leaves. Let cool, then strain into an airtight 1-pint glass container. Seal the container and store in the refrigerator for up to 1 month.

Named after the Fleetwood Mac song, this cocktail by A-K Hada, general manager of Existing Conditions, will set martini fans' hearts aflutter. The drink's pearlescent hue, along with its cool, fresh botanicals, are reminiscent of the idyllic land in the drink's namesake song. A-K splits the base between sake-based umeshu (plum liqueur) and gin, with a touch of aloe liqueur. Her inspiration was culinary: *ume shiso maki,* a sushi roll stuffed with ume (pickled plum) and shiso that is often served at the end of an *omakase* meal at her favorite Japanese restaurant.

SILVER SPRINGS

1 fresh shiso leaf

1 slice English cucumber

1¾ ounces Kamoizumi umeshu

1¼ ounces Hendrick's gin

1 teaspoon Chareau aloe liqueur (or substitute green Chartreuse)

Garnish: a cucumber coin pierced by a fresh shiso leaf

SERVES

ONE

MY FRIENDS

Muddle the shiso leaf and slice of cucumber in a mixing glass. Add the umeshu, gin, and aloe liqueur with ice and stir. Fine-strain into a chilled cocktail glass. Garnish with a shiso leaf curled and pulled through the center of a cucumber coin by the stem, rested on the rim of the glass.

A-K HADA, EXISTING CONDITIONS, NEW YORK, NEW YORK

SHUNGA

This mischievous pink cocktail is by Rogerio Igarashi Vaz, owner of Bar Trench, a mixology-forward cocktail bar in Tokyo. It is named after *shunga,* which literally means "spring pictures." Popular during Japan's Edo Period, it is the Japanese erotic artform of illustrated *ukiyo-e* (woodblock) prints, some subtle and suggestive, others unabashedly graphic. This sensuous and refreshing cocktail, powered by barley shochu, is a fitting homage.

1½ ounces Mizunomai barley shochu

1 ounce Cucumber and Basil Shrub (recipe follows)

1½ ounces ruby grapefruit juice

½ ounce Fever-Tree tonic water

¼ ounce La Clandestine absinthe

Garnish: cucumber slice and freshly ground black pepper

Combine the shochu, shrub, and grapefruit juice in a tumbler with ice. Top with the tonic water and gently stir. Using a barspoon, float the absinthe on top. Garnish with a cucumber slice and freshly ground black pepper.

ROGERIO IGARASHI VAZ, BAR TRENCH, TOKYO, JAPAN

CUCUMBER AND BASIL SHRUB
Makes 3½ cups

4 Japanese cucumbers, cut into small cubes

2 cups fresh basil leaves

2 cups sugar

2 cups apple cider vinegar

Combine the cucumbers, basil, and sugar in a large bowl. Cover the bowl with plastic wrap and let it rest at room temperature for 1 day. Add the vinegar, cover, and let rest for another day. Fine-strain through a cheesecloth-lined strainer into an airtight 1-quart glass container, using a wooden spoon to press against the solids and extract as much liquid as possible. Seal the container and store in the refrigerator for up to 2 weeks.

SERVES

ONE

SPUMONI

PINK PEPPERCORN SYRUP

Makes 2 cups

1¼ cups water

1¼ cups sugar

4½ tablespoons pink peppercorns, crushed

1½ teaspoons grated fresh ginger

Zest of 1 grapefruit, cut into strips with a peeler or paring knife

In a large pot, combine the water, sugar, peppercorns, ginger, and grapefruit zest and bring to a gentle boil over medium heat. Reduce the heat to low and simmer, stirring, for 20 minutes, until the sugar has dissolved. Let cool, then strain into an airtight 1-pint glass container. Seal the container and store in the refrigerator for up to 2 weeks.

This is a twist on an Italian-style cocktail, the Spumoni (Italian for "foam"), that has taken Tokyo by storm. With its origins as a cross between a Greyhound and a Garibaldi, Jon Mullen marries Campari, gin, pink peppercorn syrup, tonic, and "fluffy" grapefruit juice from a Breville juicer, as is done at Dante in Manhattan. The gin he prefers here is Neversink, which has a base of apple distillate rather than grain neutral spirit, which provides a rounder mouthfeel. Mullen had initially learned about the cocktail through the Japanese anime series *Bartender,* which aired in 2006. It tells the story of a bartending prodigy Ryu Sasakura, his drink-making virtuosity, and his impact on the lives of his guests. While virtually unknown on this side of the Pacific, the Spumoni is worth getting to know and seeing what all the hubbub is all about.

1¼ ounces Campari

½ ounce Neversink gin

¼ ounce Pink Peppercorn Syrup (recipe at left)

1½ ounces Fever-Tree Indian tonic water

Fresh grapefruit juice (made fresh with a Breville 800JEXL Juice Fountain Elite, if possible)

Garnish: cracked pink peppercorns

Combine the Campari, gin, and syrup in a tumbler over ice and gently stir. Add the tonic water, top with fresh grapefruit juice, and gently stir to combine. Garnish with cracked pink peppercorns.

JON MULLEN, BAR PISELLINO, NEW YORK, NEW YORK

SERVES

ONE

MY FRIENDS

STELLAR ESPERANZA

This cocktail was created by Yukiko Watanabe, former bartender at Sky Lounge Stellar Garden, which is ensconced on the top floor of the Prince Park Tower Tokyo with breathtaking panoramic views of the city. This includes the Tokyo Tower, a symbol of the capital that is recognized around the world. Her drink is a twist on a gin sour, with Japanese gin modified by a unique umeshu (plum liqueur) that has brandy as its base, instead of the more common sake or shochu, with an apple shrub providing balancing acidity. "Stellar" salutes the name of the bar, which itself was named for the shooting stars that are often visible from its thirty-third floor perch, and *esperanza* (meaning "hope" in Spanish) for the Light of Hope, a blue gemstone that also inspired the cocktail's color.

SERVES

ONE

Sugar, for rimming the glass

Lemon wedge, for rimming the glass

1½ ounces Suntory Roku gin

½ ounce Choya Ume Excellent umeshu (or substitute Choya Umeshu Classic)

⅓ ounce Mizkan Honey Apple Shrub

1 drop natural blue food coloring

Garnish: edible gold leaf

Rim a chilled martini glass with sugar (see page 55). Combine the gin, umeshu, shrub, and food coloring in a cocktail shaker with ice. Shake until chilled, then strain into the prepared glass. Garnish with edible gold leaf.

YUKIKO WATANABE, SKY LOUNGE STELLAR GARDEN, TOKYO, JAPAN

HOUSEMADE APPLE JAM

Makes 1½ cups

1 cup grated peeled Fuji apple

1 cup sugar

In a small saucepan, combine the apple and sugar and cook over low heat, stirring, until the sugar has completely dissolved and the mixture takes on a viscous quality from the apple pectin. Let cool, then transfer to an airtight 1-pint glass container. Seal the container and store in the refrigerator for up to 2 weeks.

Nobuaki Takahashi, owner and bartender at Recette, a revered Ginza bar, conceived of this time-travel cocktail as something he would serve to John Walker, the historical founder of Johnnie Walker Scotch whisky. The included ingredients would be sure to please Mr. Walker, including Johnnie Walker Gold Reserve, as well as aromatic Earl Grey tea that complements the peaty notes of the whisky. The cocktail is designed to excite all five senses.

1 whole almond, toasted

½ soft ume (Japanese plum)

1½ ounces Johnnie Walker Gold Reserve

1 teaspoon Housemade Apple Jam (recipe at left)

¾ ounce brewed Earl Grey tea, chilled

1 barspoon fresh lime juice

1 teaspoon cane syrup

Garnish: marshmallow and Earl Grey tea smoke

In a cocktail shaker, muddle the toasted almond and ume. Add the Johnnie Walker, jam, tea, lime juice, and cane syrup with ice and shake until chilled. Fine-strain into a cocktail glass. Using a small torch, toast a marshmallow and Earl Grey tea leaves to accompany the drink.

NOBUAKI TAKAHASHI, RECETTE, TOKYO, JAPAN

TIMELESS

SERVES

ONE

MY FRIENDS

231

TOKYO JOE

This cocktail created by Mari Kamata, beverage manager at the Peninsula Tokyo, has a cinematic inspiration. It takes its name from a 1949 noir film starring Humphrey Bogart, the first Hollywood production filmed in postwar Japan. It tells the tale of Bogart's hard-boiled character returning to Japan to check on his bar and gambling den, Tokyo Joe. He discovers his Japanese wife has divorced him in absentia, thinking he was a casualty of the war and, simultaneously, finds himself at odds with the Japanese mafia. While good ultimately triumphs, the protagonist's fate is left ambiguous.

1 ounce Bombay Sapphire gin

¾ ounce umeshu

⅓ ounce Drambuie

1 ounce cranberry juice

⅓ ounce fresh lemon juice

Combine the gin, umeshu, Drambuie, cranberry juice, and lemon juice in a cocktail shaker with ice. Shake until chilled and strain into a chilled cocktail glass.

MARI KAMATA, THE PENINSULA TOKYO, TOKYO, JAPAN

MY FRIENDS

SERVES

ONE

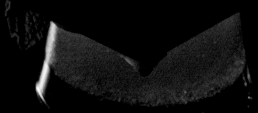

GREEN TEA–INFUSED TUMUGI

Makes 750ml

1 (750ml) bottle Tumugi

1 cup loose green tea leaves (Ureshino-cha from Saga is recommended)

Combine the Tumugi and green tea in an airtight 1-quart glass container. Cover and let stand at room temperature for 24 hours. Strain into the original Tumugi bottle and store in the pantry for up to 1 month.

TUMUGI SYRUP

Makes 1¾ cups

12 ounces Tumugi
1 cup sugar
3½ ounces water

In a small saucepan, combine the Tumugi, sugar, and water and bring to a boil over medium heat, stirring to dissolve the sugar. Let cool, then pour into an airtight 1-quart glass container. Seal the container and store in the refrigerator for up to 2 months.

Mina Ebihara, bartender at Guzzle at The SG Club in Tokyo, created this recipe to incorporate a unique style of enjoying sake, which is sometimes served with a little mound of salt on the rim of the *masu.* Its base is Tumugi, a koji-spirit introduced by the producer of iichiko shochu. The cocktail's name is a play on words on the spirit and the Japanese verb *tsumugu,* meaning to connect with and be interwoven with people, as this drink certainly encourages.

1 ounce Tumugi (or substitute iichiko Saiten shochu)

½ ounce Green Tea–Infused Tumugi (recipe at left)

⅓ ounce Tumugi Syrup (recipe at left)

1 barspoon mirin

1 barspoon yuzu juice

1 fresh shiso leaf, julienned

Garnish: grated yuzu zest and a tiny mound of salt

Combine the Tumugi, green tea–infused Tumugi, syrup, mirin, yuzu juice, and shiso leaf in a cocktail shaker with ice. Shake until chilled and fine-strain into a sake glass set in a masu or in a small stemmed wineglass. Using a Microplane, grate yuzu zest on top of the cocktail and add a tiny mound of salt.

MINA EBIHARA, GUZZLE AT THE SG CLUB, TOKYO, JAPAN

TUMUGIST

SERVES

ONE

MY FRIENDS

WAKABA

A cocktail created by Katana Kitten's exuberantly pompadoured Kodai Yamada, this highball is one of our top sellers at the bar during springtime. Its name means "new, young leaf of the season" in Japanese, and it is his take on the extremely popular Chu-Hai, which is short for Shochu Highball. The drink has a profusion of green notes and herbaceousness, yet it is simple and refreshing. Its base is equal parts iichiko Saiten shochu and French vermouth with a subtle hint of sweet basil. Carbonated tomatillo water adds an herbaceous, fruity body, and highly-carbonated soda water adds the finishing effervescent touch. Kodai garnishes this drink with fresh Thai basil, which has a sharp, peppery aroma.

Wasabi Salt (recipe follows), for rimming the glass

Lime wedge for rimming the glass

1 ounce iichiko Saiten shochu

1 ounce Dolin Blanc vermouth

1 barspoon Clear Creek Douglas fir eau-de-vie

1½ ounces carbonated Tomatillo Water (recipe follows)

½ ounce Basil Syrup (recipe follows)

Soda water, chilled

Garnish: fresh Thai basil leaf

Rim half a highball glass with wasabi salt (see page 55). Add the shochu, vermouth, eau-de-vie, tomatillo water, and basil syrup with ice and gently stir to combine. Top with chilled soda water. Garnish with a fresh Thai basil leaf.

KODAI YAMADA, KATANA KITTEN, NEW YORK, NEW YORK

WASABI SALT
Makes 2 cups

1 cup ground dehydrated fresh wasabi (see Note)

1 cup Maldon salt

Combine the salt and wasabi in a heavy-duty blender or spice grinder and grind. Transfer to an airtight 1-pint glass container. Seal the container and store in the pantry for up to 2 months.

NOTE: *Spread fresh wasabi out in a thin layer in a dehydrator and dehydrate completely. Using a heavy-duty blender, blend the dried wasabi into a powder.*

TOMATILLO WATER
Makes about 2 cups

2 pounds fresh tomatillos

Remove the husks from the tomatillos and rinse well. Juice the tomatillos using a vegetable juicer and refrigerate to allow to settle, skimming any foam off the top. Strain through a Superbag or a coffee filter into an airtight 1-pint glass container. Use a home carbonation system to carbonate the tomatillo water, and store in the refrigerator for up to 2 days.

SERVES

ONE

BASIL SYRUP

Makes 2 cups

1¼ cups water
1¼ cups sugar
10 fresh sweet basil
leaves
10 fresh Thai basil leaves

In a small saucepan,
combine the water
and sugar and bring to
a gentle simmer over
medium-high heat,
stirring to dissolve the
sugar. Remove from the
heat, add the basil leaves,
cover, and let stand
for 15 minutes. Strain
through cheesecloth
into an airtight 1-pint
glass container. Seal the
container and store in
the refrigerator for up
to 1 week.

This play on the Bamboo cocktail is courtesy of bartender Atsushi Suzuki, formerly of Savor at the SG Club in Tokyo. The drink itself has its origins in the 1890s, during the first golden age of the cocktail. It was the brainchild of Louis Eppinger, a German-born bartender who held court at the Grand Hotel in Yokohama, one of the first places to serve cocktails in Japan. Atsushi's version, which he deems a Japanese aperitif cocktail, nods to the classic recipe driven by vermouth and sherry. As a twist, he adds shochu to the mix to provide a more potent base, with rice wine vinegar providing a slight piquant note to this elegant cocktail.

1 ounce The SG Club Kome shochu (or substitute any rice shochu)

1 ounce fino sherry

$\frac{2}{3}$ ounce sweet vermouth

$\frac{1}{3}$ ounce dry vermouth

3 dashes rice vinegar

Garnish: yuzu twist

Combine the shochu, sherry, vermouths, and vinegar in a mixing glass with ice. Stir until chilled and strain into a chilled coupe. Garnish with a yuzu twist.

ATSUSHI SUZUKI, FORMERLY OF THE SG CLUB, TOKYO, JAPAN

WA-PERITIF

SERVES

ONE

MY FRIENDS

WHITE LADY

The White Lady is the defining cocktail of Hidetsugu Ueno, owner of Bar High Five in Tokyo's Ginza district and popularizer of the hard shake technique. His recipe adheres very closely to the classic specifications, as is common in cocktail bars in Ginza. If you want to practice the hard shake, this is the drink for it, and you will be rewarded with an exceptional mouthfeel. Mr. Ueno recently revealed to me how the White Lady became his signature cocktail. He had been working at Star Bar, another revered Ginza destination, and a guest asked for a White Lady, a very reasonable request. The problem was, all the bar's shakers were being used, and the only one left was an oversize shaker designed for cocktail competitions that could make up to five drinks at a time. The guest was very impressed, not only by the cocktail, but by the shaker, and when the guest inquired why Mr. Ueno used such a large shaker, to save face, Ueno told him that only a large shaker could create the tiny bubbles he was seeking. The guest not only believed this white lie, but apparently related it to everyone he knew. Suddenly, guests were coming in and demanding a White Lady made in a "big shaker." This story has followed Mr. Ueno around the world, and he apologizes for his harmless indiscretion. But it definitely demonstrates the power of storytelling in the cocktail realm.

1½ ounces Tanqueray London dry gin

½ ounce Cointreau

½ ounce fresh lemon juice

Combine the gin, Cointreau, and lemon juice in a cobbler shaker with ice. Shake until chilled, then strain into a chilled cocktail glass.

HIDETSUGU UENO, BAR HIGH FIVE, TOKYO, JAPAN

MY FRIENDS

SERVES

ONE

YOSHIMI WINS

This cocktail by Darryl D. Chan, head bartender at Bar Pleiades in New York City, is inspired by *Yoshimi Battles the Pink Robots,* an album (and eponymous song) by the Flaming Lips. A twist on a classic twentieth-century cocktail, the drink's name refers to the song's fierce protagonist, Yoshimi, whom Darryl salutes with an equally vibrant measure of shiso and wasabi. He imagines having this drink with Yoshimi after being behind the bar with her and battling off a busy service.

1½ ounces Krogstad Festlig aquavit

½ ounce Campari

½ ounce Shiso Syrup (recipe follows)

¾ ounce fresh lemon juice

5 drops Iki Japanese bitters or Bittermens Hellfire Habanero Shrub

Garnish: lemon twist

Combine the aquavit, Campari, syrup, lemon juice, and bitters with ice in a cocktail shaker. Shake and double-strain into a chilled Nick & Nora glass. Garnish with a lemon twist.

DARRYL D. CHAN, BAR PLEIADES, NEW YORK, NEW YORK

SHISO SYRUP
Makes 2 cups

1¼ cups sugar
1¼ cups water
20 fresh shiso leaves

In a small saucepan, combine the sugar and water and bring to a boil over medium-high heat, stirring to dissolve the sugar. Remove the pot from the heat, add the shiso leaves, cover, and steep for 20 minutes. Strain into an airtight 1-pint glass container. Seal the container and store in the refrigerator for up to 2 weeks.

SERVES

ONE

This cocktail was created by Chicago libations luminary Julia Momose of Kumiko, the acclaimed bar and restaurant that has earned a Michelin star. Julia's drink salutes yuzu, the fragrant Japanese citrus fruit, and chocolate, or *choco* in Japanese. While it is difficult to classify the cocktail, it will no doubt appeal to martini drinkers and aficionados of all things stirred and spirit-forward. The fact that its foundation is lower-proof shochu preserves the drink's delicate flavors and enables guests to perhaps indulge in more than one.

YUZU CHOCO

1½ ounces barley shochu (Yanagita Koma shochu or iichiko Silhouette shochu are recommended, both of which are at the classic 25% ABV)

1 ounce yuzushu (Joto or Umenoyado brands are recommended)

¼ ounce Tempus Fugit crème de cacao

1 teaspoon Suze gentiane liqueur

Garnish: lemon twist and an interwoven lemon twist

SERVES ONE

MY FRIENDS

Combine the shochu, yuzushu, crème de cacao, and Suze with ice in a mixing glass. Stir and strain over cracked or cubed ice in a rocks glass. Express a lemon twist over the cocktail and discard, and garnish with an interwoven lemon twist.

JULIA MOMOSE, KUMIKO, CHICAGO, ILLINOIS

PART

KATANA

BAR SNACKS

KITTEN

THREE

The bar snacks at Katana Kitten have proven to be enormously popular, perhaps because they are unabashedly fun (and, of course, delicious). Our concept was to take traditional American bar snacks and transform them with Japanese flavors and ingredients that might be new to our guests. By blending the familiar with the surprising, we take our guests on little gastronomic adventures, while keeping them in their comfort zone. The recipes that follow have been scaled for the home kitchen and are ordered from lighter to more substantial dishes.

BUT BEFORE OUR DEEP DIVE into the recipes, no discussion of Japanese gastronomy
would be complete without addressing umami,
the fifth taste that joins sweet, sour, salty,
and bitter. Characterized as savory, it can
be found in a wide array of foods and ingredients, including Parmesan cheese, toma-
toes, soy sauce, mushrooms, seaweed, and
miso. Scientifically speaking, they are
amino acids called glutamic acids (or glutamates). Japanese chemists were the first
to isolate them, which led to the creation of
monosodium glutamate (MSG). As you will see
in the recipes, we try to incorporate as many
naturally umami-rich ingredients as possible
into our dishes to create symphonies of flavor. So if a "secret sauce" of deliciousness
exists, it is umami.

As with the cocktails, focus on a dish or two
that you want to re-create and purchase the
ingredients accordingly. There is no need
to buy every single ingredient listed in the
Japanese pantry described later. If you don't
have a Japanese grocery nearby, the ingredients can be purchased online, but plan ahead
and factor in the shipping time.

Add the mustard, mayonnaise, miso, salt, and pepper to the bowl with the egg yolks and whip to combine. Fill the halved egg whites with the yolk mixture. Arrange on a serving plate or platter and top with ponzu-cured salmon roe, chives, and uni, if desired.

Deviled eggs are enjoying a renaissance in the US, especially on bar menus. Perhaps it is because of their retro appeal, or maybe it is because they create a wonderful platform for extra toppings, and then again, their popularity might stem from their embodying a high-low dynamic of being a little fancy, while totally accessible. We knew we wanted them on Katana Kitten's menu and we proudly pulled out all the stops to make them extremely tasty using Japanese *karashi* mustard, Kewpie mayonnaise, and miso, not to mention their elegant toppings, which include salmon roe, chives, and uni, upon a guest's request.

6 large eggs

1 teaspoon Japanese karashi mustard

3 tablespoons Kewpie mayonnaise

1 tablespoon white miso paste

1½ teaspoons salt

1½ teaspoons freshly ground black pepper

Optional toppings: ponzu-cured salmon roe, fresh chives, and uni

Place the eggs in a pan filled with cold water and bring to a boil over high heat, then reduce the heat to medium-low and simmer for 11 minutes. Remove from the heat and transfer the eggs to an ice bath to cool. Peel the eggs, cut them in half lengthwise, and transfer the yolks to a medium bowl. Set the whites aside.

DEVILED EGGS

SERVES

FOUR

CHARRED JAPANESE EGGPLANT

In this dish, Chef Cyed Adraincem marries two classic Japanese dishes, *nasu nibitashi* (roasted eggplant with dashi sauce) and *agedashi tofu* (a fried tofu dish served with a warm dashi broth). It is a highly savory, two-fisted vegetarian option that our guests have come to crave.

2 Japanese eggplants, halved lengthwise

2 tablespoons vegetable oil

Salt and freshly ground black pepper

Frying oil, canola is recommended

1 (14-ounce) package extra-firm tofu, drained and cut into ½-inch cubes

Chili Ponzu Sauce (recipe follows), for serving

In a bowl, toss the eggplant halves with the oil and season with salt and pepper. Heat a large sauté pan over medium heat. Place the seasoned eggplant halves flesh-side down in the hot pan and cook until charred and caramelized, around 5 minutes. Flip the halves and cook the skin side until charred and caramelized, around 5 minutes. Cut into bite-size pieces.

Fill a high-sided large saucepan with frying oil to a depth of 3 to 5 inches and heat over high heat to 350°F. Add the tofu and deep-fry until golden brown and crispy.

In a serving bowl, combine the cooked eggplant with the tofu and serve with Chili Ponzu Sauce.

CHILI PONZU SAUCE

Makes 2 cups

1 cup soy sauce

1 cup rice vinegar

½ garlic clove, grated

¼ cup Lao Gan Ma Chili Crisp Sauce

Combine the soy sauce, vinegar, garlic, and crisp sauce in a heavy-duty blender and blend until smooth. Pour into an airtight 1-pint glass container. Seal the container and store in the refrigerator for up to 1 month.

SERVES

ONE

RED MISO DRESSING

Makes ¼ cup

3 tablespoons Kewpie mayonnaise

1 tablespoon red miso paste

Combine the mayonnaise and red miso in an airtight glass container. Seal the container and store in the refrigerator for up to 5 days.

TOFU TAHINI

Makes ½ cup

¼ (14-ounce) package extra-firm tofu

1 tablespoon tahini

1 tablespoon fresh lemon juice

1 tablespoon white soy sauce

1 tablespoon finely chopped scallions

1 teaspoon shio kombu

½ teaspoon grated fresh ginger

¼ teaspoon minced garlic

Combine the tofu, tahini, lemon juice, soy sauce, scallions, shio kombu, ginger, and garlic in a blender and pulse until smooth and fully mixed. Transfer to an airtight 1-cup glass container. Seal the container and store in the refrigerator for up to 2 days.

This recipe was inspired by one of my favorite bars in Tokyo, Little Smith, and their hospitable gesture of serving carrot and cucumber sticks so that a guest need not drink on an empty stomach. Their version is served with miso mayonnaise, which is simply miso (white or red) mixed with Kewpie mayonnaise, a dip we all grew up on in Japan. We build on this classic recipe with an accompanying Tofu Tahini.

Seasonal greenmarket vegetables, including romaine lettuce, cucumbers, carrots, radishes, radicchio, and zucchini

Red Miso Dressing (recipe at left)

Tofu Tahini (recipe at left)

Rinse all the vegetables and pat them dry. Cut and plate the vegetables. Serve with Red Miso Dressing and Tofu Tahini alongside for dipping.

MARKET CRUDITÉS

SERVES

ONE

KATANA KITTEN BAR SNACKS

255

GRIDDLED CAROLINA WHITE PRAWN

Shrimp are immensely popular in Japan, and large prawns are particularly prized. We procure large Gulf prawns, one of the most sought-after seafoods in the US. While our recipe is straightforward, there is a trick to maximizing the flavor of the shrimp: a marinade of Thai shrimp paste. Note that you can save the shrimp head to prepare the Umami Situation on page 268.

1 large (U5) head-on Gulf prawn

Shrimp paste, enough to coat the prawn

Salt

½ lemon

Clean the prawn by removing the shell below the head and above the tail and devein the prawn. Coat the prawn with shrimp paste and marinate for at least a couple of hours or up to overnight in the refreigerator.

Preheat the oven to 400°F.

Sprinkle salt evenly over the prawn and cook in an oven-safe sauté pan over medium-high heat for about 5 minutes on each side. Transfer to the oven and cook for about 1½ minutes, until cooked through. Squeeze the lemon juice over the prawn and serve immediately.

SERVES

ONE

YUZU KOSHO MAYONNAISE

Makes ¾ cup

¾ cup Kewpie mayonnaise
1 tablespoon yuzu kosho

Combine the mayonnaise and yuzu kosho in an airtight 1-cup glass container. Seal the container and store in the refrigerator for up to 1 week.

This dish gives the beloved American comfort food a true Japanese makeover. It was created by Katana Kitten's chef Nick Sorrentino together with James Tune. We sell an incredible number of them every day. What sets it apart is a special mayonnaise made with *yuzu kosho,* a condiment made from Japanese green chiles, yuzu peel, and salt.

1 tablespoon butter, at room temperature

2 slices Japanese milk bread

1½ tablespoons Yuzu Kosho Mayonnaise (recipe at left)

½ teaspoon black sesame seeds

1 (4-inch) square nori sheet

3 tablespoons grated Muenster cheese

Spread the butter on one side of each slice of bread and spread the mayonnaise on the other side of each slice. Sprinkle black sesame seeds on both sides with mayonnaise. Place the nori sheet on the mayonnaise-covered side of one slice, then top with the grated cheese, and finished with the second slice of bread, mayo-side down. In a pan, cook the sandwich over medium-low heat until it is golden brown and the cheese has fully melted, about 4 minutes on each side.

KATANA KITTEN GRILLED CHEESE

SERVES

ONE

MORTADELLA KATSU SANDO

SERVES ONE

AS AN ENTRÉE OR 4 AS A SHARED APPETIZER

Our culinary pièce de résistance on our bar menu is the Mortadella Katsu Sando. The inspiration here is *hamu katsu,* a panko-crusted ham steak that is enormously popular in Japan. We thought why not substitute ham with mortadella, one of the ultimate expressions of porky deliciousness? It worked like a charm, and we sell a ton of the sandwiches that are dressed with Dijon mustard and a housemade traditional tonkatsu sauce.

Frying oil (canola recommended)

1 (½-inch-thick) slice mortadella

½ cup all-purpose flour

1 egg, beaten

1 cup Japanese panko bread crumbs

2 slices Japanese milk bread

1½ teaspoons Dijon mustard

1 tablespoon Tonkatsu Sauce (recipe follows)

Fill a high-sided saucepan with frying oil to a depth of 2 to 3 inches and heat over high heat to 350°F.

Dredge the mortadella in the flour, dip it in the beaten egg, and dredge in panko bread crumbs. Add the mortadella to the hot oil and fry until golden brown, about 1½ to 2 minutes for each side, flipping once.

Spread the mustard over one slice of Japanese milk bread and the tonkatsu sauce over the other. Place the fried mortadella between the two bread slices, then cut the edges of the crust to form a square. Cut into four square pieces and serve.

TONKATSU SAUCE

Makes 2½ cups

2 teaspoons Japanese karashi mustard

2 cups ketchup

½ cup Worcestershire sauce

2½ tablespoons soy sauce

Combine the mustard, ketchup, Worcestershire, and soy sauce in a blender and blend until fully incorporated. Pour into an airtight 2½-cup glass container. Seal the container and store in the refrigerator for up to 2 weeks.

SWEET-AND-SOUR SCALLION SAUCE

Makes 3 cups

2 cups rice vinegar

1 cup mirin

½ cup sugar

¼ cup white soy sauce

2 scallions, finely chopped

1½ teaspoons sambal

1½ teaspoons chopped fresh ginger

½ garlic clove, crushed

1 tablespoon potato starch

In a medium saucepan, combine the vinegar, mirin, sugar, soy sauce, scallions, sambal, ginger, and garlic. Bring to a simmer over medium heat, stirring to dissolve the sugar. Turn off the heat and let cool. Transfer to an airtight glass container, cover and refrigerate overnight. Return the sauce to a pot, heat it over medium-low heat, stir in the potato starch, then remove from the heat and let cool. Pour into an airtight glass container. Seal the container and store in the refrigerator for up to 1 week.

Starting close to home, our top-selling Fujimi Crispy Chicken is actually inspired by my Fujimi *obaachan* (maternal grandma), right down to the soy-garlic-and-sake marinade, as well as her signature Sweet-and-Sour Scallion Sauce. It was something that I grew up eating. Fujimi is the name of her town in Nagano, not far from Minowa. I'm very proud to serve the dish and our guests adore it.

½ teaspoon grated fresh ginger

¼ garlic clove, minced

1 teaspoon mirin

1 teaspoon sake

1 teaspoon soy sauce

½ pound boneless, skinless chicken thighs, cut into bite-size chunks

Frying oil (canola recommended)

½ cup potato starch

Sweet-and-Sour Scallion Sauce (recipe at left)

In a medium bowl, whisk together the ginger, garlic, mirin, sake, and soy sauce. Add the chicken and marinate for a couple of hours in the refrigerator.

Fill a high-sided large saucepan with oil to a depth of 3 to 5 inches and heat over high heat to 350°F. Toss the marinated chicken thighs in the potato starch. Add the chicken to the hot oil and deep-fry until crispy and cooked through, around 4 to 5 minutes. Place on skewers and serve with Sweet-and-Sour Scallion Sauce.

FUJIMI CRISPY CHICKEN

MAKES

TWO

SKEWERS

THE TERIYAKI BURGER

McDonald's is famous for their international in-market exclusive offerings tailored to suit local tastes that never make it stateside. McDonald's in Japan is no exception, offering a teriyaki burger. In Japan, I ate more than my fair share of these beefy delights, which have inspired my own version, complete with our own teriyaki sauce. The addition of the pineapple slice harkens back to my days delivering pizzas in Japan, where our Hawaiian version had the fruity topping, along with mayonnaise and teriyaki sauce. I know this combination is controversial in the pizza world, but it really works well on this burger.

1 (5-ounce) ground beef patty

Salt

1 Martin's potato sandwich roll

1½ teaspoons Kewpie mayonnaise

1 lettuce leaf

1 tomato slice

1 shiso leaf

1 tablespoon House Teriyaki Sauce (recipe follows)

1 slice Pickled Pineapple (recipe follows)

Sprinkle each side of the patty with salt. Cook in a skillet to your preferred doneness and set aside.

Toast the bun and spread mayonnaise on each side. Build the sandwich with lettuce, a tomato slice, a shiso leaf, the cooked patty, the teriyaki sauce, and the pineapple.

HOUSE TERIYAKI SAUCE

Makes 3 cups

1 cup soy sauce

1 cup Kombu-Infused Sake (recipe follows)

1 cup mirin

½ cup sugar

1 teaspoon agar-agar (Kanten Papa brand, if available)

In a saucepan, combine the soy sauce, sake, mirin, and sugar and heat over medium-low heat, stirring to dissolve the sugar. Reduce the heat to low and cook to burn off the sake's alcohol, concentrate the flavor, and thicken the texture, around 15 to 20 minutes. Remove from the heat, stir in the agar-agar, and allow to cool. Pour into an airtight 1-quart glass container. Seal the container and store in the refrigerator for up to 1 month.

SERVES

ONE

PICKLED PINEAPPLE

Makes 2¼ cups

1 (20-ounce) can Dole pineapple slices in syrup

¾ cup white wine vinegar

1 tablespoon kosher salt

1 tablespoon Szechuan peppercorns

Drain the syrup from the sliced pineapple into a small saucepan—it should be about 1½ cups. Add the vinegar, salt, and peppercorns. Bring to a simmer over medium heat, then let cool. Place the drained pineapple slices in an airtight 1-quart glass container. Pour the cooled pickling brine over the pineapple, cover, refrigerate and let pickle for 2 to 3 days. Store in the refrigerator for up to 1 month.

KOMBU-INFUSED SAKE

Makes about 3 cups

1 (720ml) bottle sake

1 sheet kombu

Combine the sake and kombu in an airtight 1-quart glass container. Let stand for 5 days, then remove the kombu. Pour into the original sake bottle and store in the refrigerator for up to 3 months.

NORI
FRIES

Our Nori Fries salute Japan's hugely popular snack, nori chips, and with the addition of the optional curry sauce, it is like poutine meets Irish curry chips by way of New Jersey disco fries. They are a perennial bestseller at Katana Kitten. The inspiration is a classic Japanese potato chip flavor, *nori-shio,* a combination of dried seaweed and salt. The crinkle cut of the fries do a great job of holding on to this savory seasoning.

Frying oil, enough to create a depth of 3 to 5 inches in a pot

2 cups crinkle-cut potatoes

1 tablespoon *aonori* (dried seaweed)

½ teaspoon sea salt

Fill a high-sided large saucepan with frying oil to a depth of 3 to 5 inches and heat over medium heat to 350°F. Add the potatoes and fry until golden brown and crispy. Drain and toss with the aonori and salt.

SERVES

ONE

UMAMI SITUATION

This is an off-menu item at Katana Kitten that our guests are absolutely obsessed with, that pairs two potables with a bit of a culinary twist: a Shrimp Head Shot served alongside a shot of shochu. A grilled shrimp head in a drink might seem bizarre to Western sensibilities, but in truth, the head is the tastiest part of the crustacean and is used in many classic seafood stocks around the world. At Katana Kitten, we prepare it very theatrically for our guests, no matter how busy the bar is. You basically take a grilled shrimp head, place it in a handheld citrus juicer with a lemon wedge, and give it a good squeeze. A drizzle of *junmai* sake is added. The concentrated flavors create a real umami explosion in your mouth. This is accompanied by a shot of iichiko Saiten, a higher-proof barley shochu that washes it down, yet also activates the taste buds to create a very long finish for the Shrimp Head Shot. The shrimp head is then deep-fried and topped with sea salt and freshly ground sansho pepper.

SERVES ONE

Shrimp Head Shot (recipe follows)

1 shot iichiko Saiten shochu

Fried Shrimp Head (recipe follows)

Serve two shot glasses, one filled with Shrimp Head Shot and one filled with iichiko Saiten, with the fried shrimp head on the side.

SHRIMP HEAD SHOT
Serves 1

1 shrimp head (reserved from the Griddled Carolina White Prawn, page 256)

¼ lemon wedge

Sea salt

½ ounce junmai sake

Put the shrimp head and a lemon wedge dipped in sea salt in a handheld citrus squeezer and press to squeeze all the juice together. Reserve the pressed shrimp head to make the Fried Shrimp Head (recipe follows). Drizzle the junmai sake into this mixture. Pour into a shot glass.

FRIED SHRIMP HEAD

Serves 1

Frying oil (canola recommended)

1 pressed shrimp head (reserved from the Shrimp Head Shot)

Sea salt

Freshly ground sansho pepper

Fill a high-sided medium saucepan with oil to a depth of 3 to 5 inches and heat over high heat to 350°F. Add the shrimp head to the hot oil and deep-fry until crispy. Remove the head from the oil, drain on paper towels, season with salt and sansho pepper to taste, and serve with the shots.

THE JAPANESE PANTRY

For those who are hungry to try the cocktail and food recipes in this book, the following is an overview of ingredients that will come in handy for your adventures. Since the time of my arrival in the US a little over a decade ago, authentic Japanese ingredients have become far easier to obtain. There are a growing number of Japanese groceries or Asian markets that are, happily, proliferating. The ingredients that follow constitute a basic list of Japanese pantry staple items. There is no need to go out and purchase every ingredient, just the ones you need for the recipes that capture your imagination and palate.

AMAZAKE: A sweet sake that traditionally contains no alcohol.

AN OR ANKO: A paste of ground red mung beans, often sweetened with sugar. In Japanese sweets, it is a ubiquitous stuffing for *anpan* (sweet bread buns), *mochi* (rice cakes) or *taiyaki* (a waffle-like cake, often shaped like a fish). Available as a smooth (*koshian*) or chunky (*tsubuan*) paste, it can also be made into a sweet soup (*oshiruko*). *Shiroan* is produced from white beans while other variations are made from chestnuts or sweet potatoes.

AWAMORI: A "cousin" of shochu, distilled from Thai rice that relies on black *koji* to convert the rice's starch into fermentable sugar, a process known as saccharification. This spirit can only be produced in Okinawa to be legally called *awamori.* While somewhat rarer than shochu, it can be procured in the US.

AZUKI OR ADZUKI: A red mung bean.

BIRU: Beer is a universal and ubiquitous beverage in Japan, with major producers who are quite familiar to Americans, such as Asahi, Kirin, Sapporo, and Suntory. Their beers are uniformly well-made pilsner-style lagers. In recent years, *ji-bīru* (local craft beers) have made inroads. In fact, my younger brother, Kota, is employed as a brewer in Nagano, near our hometown. His brewery, Minami Shinshu Beer, produces traditional yet unique brews, including many in the German style.

BUTTERFLY PEA FLOWER: A Southeast Asian flower, it is made into a tisane, or herbal tea, that magically turns from dark blue to intense violet when acids are added, so it can add a dramatic, transformative touch to sour-style cocktails. It is also available in powdered form.

CALPICO: A beloved soft drink in Japan (locally branded CALPIS) that has a mildly yogurt-like taste and milky appearance.

DAIKON: Literally meaning "big root," daikon is a large winter radish that is native to East, Southeast, and South Asia. In Japan, it is often pickled or grated. The leaves can also be pickled. Daikon radish sprouts often adorn sashimi.

DASHI: A clear, savory broth that is a foundational ingredient in Japanese cuisine. Dashi can be found in miso soup and various noodle broths; it is also used as a flavoring agent to impart notes of umami. The most popular version is a broth derived from kombu (dried kelp) and *katsuobushi* (dried and smoked shavings of skipjack or bonito tuna). Other dashi is made from shiitake mushrooms or *niboshi* (dried sardines or other fish). There are numerous prepared dashi products available on the market—from powders and liquid concentrates—which are often mostly MSG. They are serviceable, but it goes without saying that homemade from scratch is best.

EDAMAME: Young soybean pods blanched in salted boiling water, a favorite appetizer in Japanese restaurants.

EGGS: Eggs are a mainstay of the Japanese kitchen and are celebrated in dishes like *chawanmushi,* a savory steamed egg custard, which my grandma masterly prepared, as well as *omuraisu,* an elaborate omelet stuffed with ketchup-tinged ham fried rice. In addition, raw eggs are widely consumed in Japan without fear of salmonella.

FURIKAKE: A seasoning for sprinkling on rice and other dishes made from any combinations of seaweed, sesame seeds, dried fish, sugar, and salt.

GARI: A palate cleanser for sushi, *gari* is young ginger sliced thinly and marinated in vinegar and sugar.

GOBO: Also known as burdock root, it is a tuber used in classic dishes such as *kinpira gobo,* which is *gobo* braised with julienned carrots, fried tofu, and sesame seeds.

GOMA: This refers to sesame seeds, which the Japanese consume in vast quantities. *Shiro goma* (white sesame) has the mildest flavor and is often used as a salad garnish that imparts texture without too much flavor. In contrast, *kuro goma* (black sesame) has a pronounced nutty flavor and is used in marinades and even desserts. A popular furikake variation combines it with salt. *Gomaabura* (sesame oil) is also a foundational ingredient in many vegetable dishes, with chili-spiced versions also quite popular.

HINOKI: A kind of cypress tree that grows extensively in Central Japan. It is renowned for its top-quality timber that is used as a construction material, as well as for *masu,* the traditional wooden box used in sake service.

KABOSU: A Japanese citrus fruit related to yuzu that has its origins in China. Cultivated widely in Oita Prefecture, it has sharp notes of acidity and often takes the place of vinegar in Japanese cuisine. Don't knock yourself out trying to find it, as it is very rare in the US, so I prefer using sudachi or yuzu instead.

KANTEN: Agar-agar, a jelly-like substance derived from *tengusa,* an algae. As an ingredient, *kanten* can be used to prepare vegan-friendly gelatins.

KARASHI: A variety of Japanese mustard that is often sold as a powder to be mixed with water. *Karashi* is a key condiment for *tonkatsu* (Japan's beloved pork cutlet) and many other fried dishes. It is part of the ever-popular Mortadella Katsu Sando (page 260) at Katana Kitten.

KATSUOBUSHI: Skipjack or bonito tuna that is smoked, dried, and shaved into flakes that are then used to make dashi, the foundational savory broth of Japanese cooking.

KINAKO: A flour made from roasted soybeans. With a nut-like flavor, it is a traditional topping of *mochi.*

KINOME LEAF: This fragrant herb from the sansho pepper plant has a distinct, sharp aroma.

KOMBU: Dried kelp that is widely used to make dashi, Japanese cuisine's basic broth. There are dozens of varieties of kombu throughout Japan, with the highest-quality sourced in Hokkaido.

KOMESU: Rice vinegar that has a sweet note from its base of rice. It is often used in *sunomono,* a vegetable salad, and as a means of perking up flavors in dishes.

KONNYAKU: A gelling agent derived from the Devil's Tongue yam that is handy for use in vegan applications.

KURUMI: Japanese walnuts.

LEMONGRASS: An aromatic tropical plant with long stalks that is related to grass and has a pronounced lemon scent. It is used throughout Asia, the Middle East, and Africa and jazzes up recipes like Thailand's *tom yum* soup.

LIME LEAF: These fragrant leaves are essential in Thai and Southeast Asian cooking and can be purchased fresh, dried, or frozen.

MIRIN: A cooking wine similar to sake, but lower in proof and with a higher sugar content. Mirin is a key ingredient in many dishes, including teriyaki sauce.

MISO: A paste made of soybeans and other grains that have been fermented with *koji,* the same benevolent mold-inoculated rice used to brew sake. Miso mixed with dashi creates basic miso soup. *Shiromiso* (white miso) is the most predominant in Western Japan, with *akamiso* (red miso) getting its ruddy color and more assertive flavor from aging. Miso finds its way into numerous Japanese dishes.

MIZUNA: A leaf that is delicate with a slight peppery taste.

MONOSODIUM GLUTAMATE (MSG): A ubiquitous flavor-enhancing agent used in food production in Japan and the US. In 1908, amino acids called glutamic acids (or glutamates) were isolated from kombu (seaweed) by Professor Kikunae Ikeda, a chemist and instructor at Tokyo Imperial University, who coined the term umami, a savory taste. Ikeda ultimately patented his discovery as monosodium glutamate (MSG). While MSG often gets a bad rap in the US, this has not been supported by scientific evidence and the ingredient has since received the endorsement of culinary stars like chef David Chang and New Yorker food writer Helen Rosner.

MUSHROOMS: Mushrooms are elemental in Japanese cuisine and include enoki (long white), *eringi* (king trumpet), *kikurage* (wood ear), maitake (hen of the woods), matsutake (pine) and, of course, shiitake, which is now popular in the US as well.

NORI: Sheets of a dried edible seaweed that, when toasted, form the outside of sushi rolls (*yaki nori*). The production of nori is similar to paper. The seaweed is harvested, then finely chopped. The pulp is then poured as a thin layer into screened blocks, where they dry into sheets.

PANDAN LEAF: These are the leaves of a tropical plant that impart a funky, fragrant note to dishes and beverages. They are popular in cuisines throughout South and Southeast Asia.

PANKO: Japanese bread crumbs that are used in tempura (fried shrimp and vegetables) and *tonkatsu* (pork cutlet) preparations.

POMELO: This is the largest citrus fruit out there and it looks like a really oversize grapefruit with a distinct flavor, especially the zest. It is popular in South and Southeast Asia. Pomelos with white flesh are sweet, while those with pink are sour.

PONZU: A condiment made by combining *katsuo* or *kombu dashi,* soy sauce, and then adding a citrus juice: *kabosu, sudachi,* or yuzu. It is often an accompaniment to sashimi and *shabu-shabu,* a highly popular DIY hotpot dish.

RAKKYO: Japanese scallions whose bulbs are often pickled.

RICE: Hundreds of varieties of rice are cultivated throughout Japan, with Koshihikari being the most prevalent. Rice seedlings are transplanted to the fields in May, with the harvest occurring in the fall. *Hakumai* is polished white rice and *genmai* is unpolished brown rice.

SAKE: Japan's "rice wine" that is brewed like beer, yet drinks more like a white wine. While sparkling sake has been introduced in recent years, sake is traditionally a still beverage, which is far more common. Other kinds of sake include *nigori,* which has a cloudy appearance. This is because it's unfiltered and retains suspended rice particles. Another is *namazake,* a type that is unpasteurized and prized for its fresh flavors. The delicate and perishable nature of *namazake* means it should always be kept refrigerated and consumed once the bottle is opened, as should all sake.

SAMBAL: A chile paste that originated in Indonesia and has spread to Malaysia, Singapore, Brunei, and Sri Lanka, as well as internationally. It is often enriched with shrimp paste, lime juice, and aromatics, like ginger and garlic.

SANSAI: A term meaning "mountain vegetables," encompassing a vast array of young plants, greens, and shoots with very short growing seasons, making them especially prized. They include *zenmai* (royal ferns), *nobiru* (red garlic), *kogomi* (fiddlehead ferns) and others. It is common to prepare them as tempura or sprinkled on soba noodles.

SANSHO PEPPER: A Japanese pepper that is often included in shichimi blends. Its leaves, called *kinome,* have a flavor that is a cross between citrus and pepper.

SHICHIMI TOGARASHI: An amalgamation of seven spices, with red chiles as the base, that is often used to add zest to soups or noodle dishes.

SHIO: The Japanese's reverence for salt harkens back to it being one of the offerings to Shinto spirits and a means of purification. Even today, restaurants in Japan have little conical mounds of salt at their front door to signal purity and attract a good clientele. Salt plays a key role in pickling vegetables, dehydrating fish, and drawing out water to concentrate umami in meat, fish, and vegetables. All domestic salt in Japan is sea salt, given that the country is an archipelago of islands touched by five seas that are never too far away. There are innumerable salts flavored with citrus, vegetables, dashi, smoke, red wine, and more.

SHIO KOJI: A condiment, flavor enhancer, and meat tenderizer that is powered by *koji* to enzymatically break down proteins. It brings sweet, salty, and fermented flavor notes.

SHIO KOMBU: A traditional Japanese snack of dried kelp that is seasoned with soy sauce, mirin, and sugar.

SHISO: A perilla leaf that is part of the mint family, shiso has an unmistakable flavor, described by some as mint meeting basil. Fresh green shiso, also known as *ōba,* is often used to cradle sashimi, and *akajiso,* red leaves, are prized for their coloring ability, especially for pickled ume.

SHOCHU: Japan's national spirit can be distilled from rice, sweet potatoes, barley, buckwheat, brown sugar, or other ingredients. Each lends the resulting shochu a distinct and discernible flavor profile. *Honkaku shochu* is distilled only once from a single ingredient and is considered artisanal.

SHOYU: Japanese soy sauce, an indispensable condiment that is fermented from soybeans, wheat, salt, and *koji.* The most popular style is *koikuchi* (dark/regular), followed by *usukuchi* (lighter), which is saltier and imparts less color to a dish.

Tamari, the forerunner of today's soy sauce, reflects the original product from China that was introduced to Japan. Traditionally, tamari contains little to no wheat, so it can potentially be suitable for those with gluten sensitivities; be sure to check with the manufacturer. Crystallized shoyu is made by boiling down soy sauce until it forms crystals. It is then used as a sprinkled condiment, like salt.

SHUNGIKU: Edible chrysanthemum leaves are used in dishes like shabu-shabu and *sukiyaki*. They impart a pleasantly fresh and sharp note.

SIMPLE SYRUP: A key mixological ingredient comprised of one part granulated sugar to one part water that is mixed together until dissolved (see page 56 for the recipe).

SOBA: Literally meaning "buckwheat," soba generally applies to buckwheat noodles typically eaten cold and dipped in a *tsuyu*, a savory sauce.

SOFT DRINKS: Japan has a very vibrant soda and soft drink culture with an unfathomable number of brands and variations. There are two that are both very popular and hold particular nostalgic appeal for me. The first is Calpico, a soft drink made from non-fat milk with a mild, yogurt-like flavor. The second is Ramune, a carbonated lemon-lime soft drink. What is most distinctive about Ramune is its packaging: a glass marble keeps the carbonation in place and has to be pushed down into the bottle to allow the soda to flow.

SUDACHI: A very sour citrus fruit cultivated in Tokushima Prefecture. It is believed to be a cross between yuzu and an orange varietal.

SUGAR: Japan definitely has a sweet tooth, as is evidenced by the wide array of sugars that are common in food and drinks. Two that stand out are *wasanbon*, a premium fine-grained sugar made from local sugarcane that is used in *wagashi*, Japan's traditional sweets, and *kokuto* (brown sugar), which hails

from Japan's western regions. *Johakuto*, white sugar, is widely used, as is *guranyuto*, a superfine sugar employed in baking, and *sanonto*, a caramelized white sugar added to stews and braised dishes.

TEA: *Camellia sinensis*, namely tea, arrived in Japan in the ninth century from China and became an integral part of its drinks culture and religious ceremonies. While there are a myriad of teas to enjoy in Japan, the following are some of the main categories.

Genmaicha is green tea with popped brown rice kernels that add a toasty note.

Hojicha is roasted green tea.

Lapsang Souchong, a black tea that hails from China's Fujian Province that has a pronounced smoky and piney aroma, since it is smoked over pinewood fires.

Matcha (powdered green tea) is when the leaves are ground into a fine powder and the entirety is mixed with hot water. It is used in sado (the Tea Ceremony), and in confections like green tea ice cream.

Mugicha (barley tea) and *Sobacha* (buckwheat tea) have pleasing roasted and nutty notes.

Sencha (green tea) is the most popular variety and its leaves are steeped to make tea.

TOFU: Originating in China, tofu is a Japanese staple and a major source of protein. Its first appearance in Japan was in the twelfth century, when it was first consumed by Buddhist monks who were forbidden to eat meat. Tofu appears in a myriad of dishes, including *abura-age*, where tofu is pressed to remove water and then deep-fried; *agedashi dofu*, which is tofu tossed in starch, deep-fried, and served in a soy and dashi sauce; and *hiyayakko*, which is chilled tofu dressed with soy sauce, bonito flakes, and/or wasabi that is popular in summer. *Yuba* are silky layers of tofu "skin" made by heating soymilk and skimming it. It can be eaten on its own with soy sauce and wasabi or used as a wrapping for other ingredients.

TSUKEMONO: These are Japanese pickles made using salt, brine, or rice bran as a preservation method. Numerous vegetables are transformed into *tsukemono*, including: ginger (*gari*), daikon (*bettarazuke*), and *nozawana*, a mustard leaf that is popular in my home prefecture of Nagano.

UME: A Japanese fruit related to plums and apricots. Umeshu, plum liqueur, is a maceration of ume in shochu, sake, or other alcoholic bases that is then sweetened with rock sugar. Umeboshi is salted and pickled ume.

WAGASHI: These are traditional Japanese sweets, which often incorporate *mochiko* (rice flour), *anko* (red bean paste), and *neri goma* (sesame paste). Some *wagashi* are available throughout Japan and year-round; others are regional and seasonal. The category as a whole has its origin as accompaniments to sado (the Tea Ceremony).

WASABI: A plant related to horseradish and mustard. Its root, when freshly ground, is used as a pungent condiment for sushi and sashimi. Most wasabi sold commercially in the US is actually ground horseradish with green coloring added. At Katana Kitten, we fly in the genuine article from Japan.

YUKARI: A salty, sour, and aromatic condiment made from red shiso leaves.

YUZU: A highly versatile citrus fruit that originated in China and came to Japan, yuzu is related to the mandarin orange. The fruit is aromatic and has a unique tang. It is often made into jams and preserves. Its fragrant zest is used to garnish various dishes. *Yuzu kosho* is a paste of ground yuzu peel, chiles, and salt; it is a bright and spicy condiment that is excellent with grilled steak, like a chimichurri sauce. *Yuzushu* is sake or shochu flavored with yuzu zest.

RESOURCE GUIDE

To source the specialty ingredients used in the recipes of this book, I highly recommend visiting a Japanese market or grocery. In recent years, cities like New York City, Los Angeles, San Francisco, and Seattle have seen a proliferation of Japanese spots, certainly many more than when I first came to the US from Japan over a decade ago.

If you've never been to a Japanese market, trust me, it is quite an experience. It is as close as you'll get to being in Japan without leaving the US and truly is a feast for the senses. You are bound to be impressed by the dazzling array of packaged foods, like ramen noodles and curries, a blizzard of riotously colorful soft drinks, candies, and sweets of every description and often a full array of fruits, vegetables, seafood, fish, and meat. In some of the larger markets, there are Japanese food stalls serving authentic street foods and snacks, and even sit-down restaurants, so you can make a whole day of your shopping outing. Depending on your state's laws, these places may also sell sake and shochu.

As always, being adventurous will be handsomely rewarded. Take it all in by cruising down each of the aisles or, if you are in a hurry, simply grab a staff member to help you find a specific item.

The following is a list of Japanese markets in major cities, as well as cities with large Japanese-American populations. They include everything from large chains to smaller-scale mom-and-pop shops. While the information is current at the time of writing, the COVID-19 pandemic has had a colossal impact on the food and beverage industry and there may be a lot of changes, so please take a moment to call ahead to confirm store hours.

If there are no Japanese groceries where you live, I'd try an Asian, Chinese, or Korean market, as they often stock Japanese goods as well. And, of course, there's always Google and the internet for tracking down and conveniently source many of these items online.

CALIFORNIA

Metro Los Angeles

Marukai
123 S. Onizuka Street,
#105
Los Angeles, CA 90012
(213) 893-7200
marukai.com

Marukai
12121 W. Pico Boulevard
Los Angeles, CA 90064
(310) 806-4120
marukia.com

Mitsuwa Marketplace
3760 S. Centinela Avenue
Los Angeles, CA 90066
(310) 398-2113
mitsuwa.com

Mitsuwa Marketplace
515 W. Las Tunas Drive
San Gabriel, CA 91776
(626) 457-2899
mitsuwa.com

Mitsuwa Marketplace
21515 Western Avenue
Torrance, CA 90501
(310) 782-0335
mitsuwa.com

Nijiya Market
2130 Sawtelle Boulevard,
#105
Los Angeles, CA 90025
(310) 575-3300
nijiya.com

Nijiya Market
2533B Pacific Coast
Highway
Torrance, CA 90505
(310) 534-3000
nijiya.com

Nijiya Market
124 Japanese Village
Plaza Mall
Los Angeles, CA 90012
(213) 680-3280
nijiya.com

Nijiya Market
2121 W. 182nd Street
Torrance, CA 90504
(310) 366-7200
nijiya.com

Nijiya Market
17869 Colima Road
City of Industry, CA 91748
(626) 913-9991
nijiya.com

Tokyo Central
1740 W. Artesia Boulevard
Gardena, CA 90248
(310) 660-6300
tokyocentral.com

Sacramento

Oto's Marketplace
4990 Freeport Boulevard
Sacramento, CA 95822
(916) 424-2398
otosmarketplace.com

San Diego

Marukai
8151 Balboa Avenue
San Diego, CA 92111
(858) 384-0248
marukai.com

Mitsuwa Marketplace
4240 Kearny Mesa Road
San Diego, CA 92111
(858) 569-6699
mitsuwa.com

Nijiya Market
3860 Convoy St., #109
San Diego, CA 92111
(858) 268-3821
nijiya.com

Metro San Francisco

Nijiya Market
1737 Post Street, #333
San Francisco, CA 94115
(415) 563-1901
nijiya.com

Metro San Jose

Marukai
19750 Stevens Creek
Boulevard
Cupertino, CA 95014
(408) 200-4850
marukai.com

Mitsuwa Marketplace
675 Saratoga Avenue
San Jose, CA 95129
(408) 255-6699
mitsuwa.com

Nijiya Market
240 Jackson Street
San Jose, CA 95112
(408) 275-6916
nijiya.com

Washington, DC Metro Area

Hana Japanese Market
2004 17th Street N.W.
Washington, DC 20009
(202) 939-8853

Maruichi Grocery
1047 Rockville Pike
Rockville, MD 20852
(301) 545-0101
maruichiusa.com

HAWAII

Honolulu

J-Shop
1513 Young Street
Honolulu, HI 96826
(808) 200-5076
jshop-hawaii.com

Marukai Wholesale Mart
2310 Kamehameha
Highway
Honolulu, HI 96819
(808) 845-5051
marukaihawaii.com

Mitsuwa
International Market
Place, #250
2330 Kalakaua Avenue
Honolulu, HI 96815
(808) 489-9020
mitsuwa.com

Nijiya Market
451 Piikoi Street
Honolulu, HI 96814
(808) 589-1121
nijiya.com

Nijiya Market
1009 University Avenue,
Suite 101
Honolulu, HI 96826
(808) 979-8977
nijiya.com

ILLINOIS

Chicago

Mitsuwa Marketplace
100 E. Algonquin Road
Arlington Heights, IL
60005
(847) 956-6699
mitsuwa.com

MASSACHUSETTS

Boston

Ebisuya Japanese
Market
65 Riverside Avenue
Medford, MA 02155
(781) 391-0012
ebisuyamarket.com

NEW YORK

New York City

Dainobu
36 W. 56th Street
New York, NY 10019
(212) 707-8525
dainobu.us

Dainobu
498 Sixth Avenue
New York, NY 10011
(212) 645-0237
dainobu.us

Dainobu
129 E. 47th Street
New York, NY 10017
(646) 838-9904
dainobu.us

Katagiri Japanese
Grocery Store
224 E. 59th Street
New York, NY 10022
(212) 755-3566
katagiri.com

Katagiri Japanese
Grocery Store
370 Lexington Avenue
New York, NY 10017
(917) 472-7025
katagiri.com

Midoriya
11 E. 17th Street
New York, NY 10003
(917) 639-3359
midoriyanyc.com

Midoriya
167 N. 9th Street
Brooklyn, NY 11211
(718) 599-4690

Sunrise Mart
4 Stuyvesant Street, 2nd
Floor
New York, NY 10003
(212) 598-3040
sunrisemart.com

Sunrise Mart
12 E. 41st Street
New York, NY 10017
(646) 380-9280
sunrisemart.com

Sunrise Mart in Japan
Village
934 3rd Avenue
Brooklyn, NY 11232
(347) 584-4579
sunrisemart.com

Sunrise Mart
494 Broome Street
New York, NY 10013
(212) 219-0033
sunrisemart.com

Taiyo Foods
45-08 44th Street
Sunnyside, NY 11104
(718) 392-2233

NEW JERSEY

Edgewater

Mitsuwa
595 River Road
Edgewater, NJ 07020
(201) 941-9113
mitsuwa.com

TEXAS

Austin

Asahi Imports
6105 Burnet Road
Austin, TX 78757
(512) 453-1850
asahiimports.com

Dallas

Mitsuwa Marketplace
100 Legacy Drive, Suite
110
Plano, TX 75023
(972) 517-1715
mitsuwa.com

Houston

Daido Market
11146 Westheimer Road
Houston, TX 77042
(713) 785-0815
facebook.com/
daidomarkethouston

WASHINGTON

Bellevue

Uwajimaya
699 120th Avenue N.E.
Bellevue, WA 98005
(425) 747-9012
uwajimaya.com

Seattle

Maruta Shoten
1024 South Bailey Street
Seattle, WA 98108
(206) 767-5002
marutashoten.com

Uwajimaya
600 5th Avenue South
Seattle, WA 98104
(206) 624-6248
uwajimaya.com

JAPANESE BARWARE, GLASSWARE, KNIVES, AND KITCHEN GEAR

Los Angeles Metro Area

Anzen Hardware
309 East 1st Street
Los Angeles, CA 90012
(213) 628-7600
facebook.com
/anzenhardware

Hitachiya USA
2509 Pacific Coast
Highway
Torrance, CA 90505
(310) 534-3136
hitachiya.com

Japanese Knife Imports
8642 Wilshire Boulevard
Beverly Hills, CA 90211
(310) 399-0300
japaneseknifeimports.com

New York City

Cocktail Kingdom
36 West 25th Street, 5th
Floor
New York, NY 10010
(212) 647-9166
cocktailkingdom.com

Korin
57 Warren Street
New York, NY 10007
(212) 587-7021
korin.com

MTC Kitchen
711 Third Avenue (enter
on 45th Street between
2nd and 3rd Avenues)
New York, NY 10017
(212) 661-3333
mtckitchen.com

Seito Trading Company
41-26 27th Street
Long Island City, NY 11101
(718) 472-5413
seito-newyork.com

Oakland

Umami Shop
4027 Broadway
Oakland, CA 94611
(510) 250-9559
umamimart.com

San Francisco

Soko Hardware
1698 Post Street
San Francisco, CA 94115
(415) 931-5510
sokohardware.com

ACKNOWLEDGMENTS

I want to thank my parents for putting everything they had into raising me and my two brothers, and for giving us the best gift—getting to grow up close to our grandparents. Their wisdom and beliefs taught and inspired me, and continue to do so every day of my life.

I also thank James Tune, Greg Boehm, Jordis Unga, and the entire Katana Kitten family for letting me be part of such a wonderful team and the bar of my dreams. Without Katana Kitten, this book would never have been written. I thank my bartender friends and colleagues, both in Japan and the US, who contributed their recipes to the book. Combined with our recipes, they really bring to life the Japanese approach to drinks. Moreover, I wouldn't be in this position without the craft bartending community at large sharing their insights and wisdom with me over the years.

I want to thank Michael Anstendig and Hanna Lee for giving me this extraordinary opportunity to share the journey of an ordinary kid like me from a small town in Japan.

My career is the result of the ethos of the hospitality industry: kindness and generosity. I'm grateful to my mentors in Japan and the US for sharing the joy of serving people, their honest advice for continuous improvement, and their encouragement to keep doing the right thing: making people happy. I'm happy to call all of my colleagues, both past and present, "family," and I'm grateful for them to be part of my life. I wouldn't be in this position without the bar and restaurant community at large sharing their insights and wisdom with me over the years.

I'd like to thank Yoshihiro Shinkawa, Kenji Hirao, Tomoaki Asai, Shigeyuki "John" Takada, Shoko Nakagawa, and Yasuyuki "Antonio" Suzuki for introducing me to the best job in the world back in Japan. It will be many years before I can even aspire to approach their commitment, dedication, and accomplishments. The art of the cocktail is still something that I endeavor to improve and perfect each and every day.

My life here in New York wouldn't have taken the same course without Paul Franich, Naren Young, Linden Pride, and, of course, Nacho Jimenez, who helped me define the best of myself at work. Making balanced drinks is not all that difficult, but this is due to all of the greats who came before us and paved the way. I wouldn't be where I am today as a bartender and a bar owner if it weren't for those who helped to define what it is to work in a bar in New York City and beyond: people like Dale DeGroff, Audrey Saunders,

Sasha Petraske, Julie Reiner, John Lermayer, and, of course, David Wondrich. I'm where I am today because of all of the many hospitality industry luminaries who make our industry what it is today.

Last, but certainly not least, I'm grateful every day for my wife, Taryn, and our daughter, Azusa, for giving me a home to share every little bit of joy in life.

I'm very fortunate to be just a bartender, but I'm, in fact, beyond lucky for having found my beautiful future wife across the counter that one night!

—Masahiro Urushido

I want to thank my parents for doing everything in their power to raise me right and providing me with advantages that they never had themselves. I owe my writing career to my mom, who enthusiastically encouraged my putting words to paper from way back in grade school and every step of the way ever since. When I told her I was co-writing a book, she was elated beyond words and supported me every step of the way. I dedicate this book to her.

It was truly an honor and a delight to work with Masahiro Urushido, whose drinks and exuberant personality I have long admired. I thank him for being so generous with his time and allowing me to take a deep dive into his life and his unique perspective. It was truly a marvelous collaboration. I also thank our contributing bartenders from Japan and the US, who absolutely dazzled us with the creativity and originality of their recipes.

As a first-time author, I especially want to thank the team at Houghton Mifflin Harcourt, including Justin Schwartz and Sarah Kwak, who embraced our book idea, nurtured it, and brought it across the finish line. We were also fortunate to work with Eric Medsker, whose exceptional photography took this book to the next level, as did the stunning book design by Laura Palese.

I raise a proverbial glass to the many reporters and writers who diligently cover Japan and Japanese-inspired bars, restaurants, cocktails, spirits, cuisine, and techniques. They have shined a vital spotlight on this tradition, as well as the wonderful authors who have documented Japan's contributions to the libations world. Their hard work helped inform and elevate our book. And, of course, I salute my literary sensei, Brad Thomas Parsons, who provided moral support and guidance throughout the writing process.

Lastly, I thank the light of my life and partner in crime, Hanna Lee, who came up with the crazy idea of incubating books, including this one, and then deputized me to write it as the first co-author and rode shotgun over the entire process. I will forever be grateful for this life-changing, enlightening experience.

—Michael Anstendig

INDEX

Note: Page references in *italics* indicate photographs.

287